ROME PRECINCTS

A curated guide to the city's
best shops, eateries, bars
and other hangouts

ROME PRECINCTS

A curated guide to the city's
best shops, eateries, bars
and other hangouts

Hardie Grant

TRAVEL

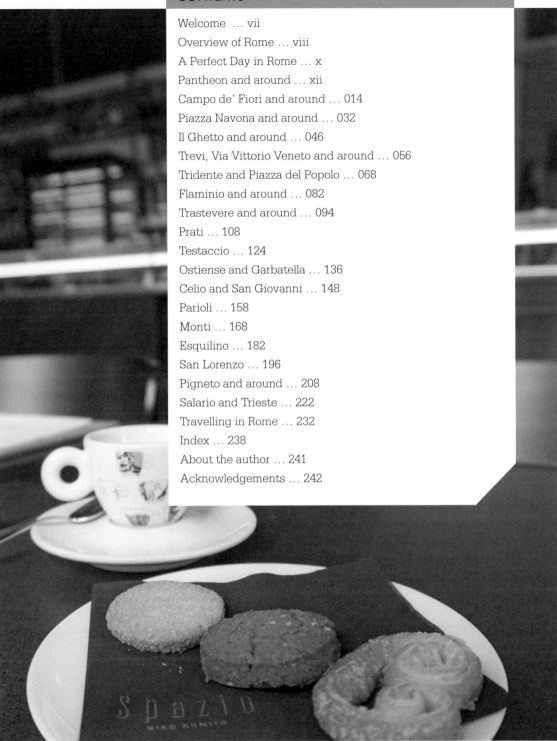

CONTENTS

Former Caput Mundi (Capital of the World) and current headquarters of Europe's most coveted boot, Rome hooks and conquers like few other cities. Ancient, culturally well-endowed and heartbreakingly handsome, its backstory reads like a top-rating Netflix biopic, filled with wolf-suckled twins, backstabbing senators, ruthless popes, rebellious artists and Hollywood starlets in search of post-war dolce vita. The result is a city in which the past is ever present, a place where trams skirt gladiatorial stadiums, shoppers browse alongside subterranean aqueducts, and art lovers swoon in the frescoed former pads of cardinals and princes.

Yet Rome is much more than crumbling ruins, frescoed chapels and selfie-snapping tourists. For its 4 million residents, Rome is a kicking, pounding metropolis in which daily life is played out with trademark Roman gusto, style and irony. *Rome Precincts* offers a porthole into *that* city, the one locals live in each day. This guide carves the Italian capital into 18 navigable precincts, each offering a selection of authentic, atmospheric and sometimes unexpected places to shop, eat and drink. It doesn't aim to cover every smashing restaurant, bar or boutique, but instead delivers an intimate, idiosyncratic snapshot to help you explore. These are the places that my amici romani (Roman friends) and I treasure.

The result is a multifaceted journey through the Eternal City, one which might see you devouring ambrosial crostate (tarts) in Il Ghetto, chatting with local designers in boho-spirited Monti, or sipping glasses of rare bubbly in a deli-cum-wine bar on a posh Parioli backstreet. Some of the recommendations are unapologetically old-school; others are fiercely progressive. Together they bring you face to face with the passions, traditions, trends and creativity that drive this city.

Of course, it would be criminal to overlook Rome's cultural muscle. And so, in between suggestions for shopping, feasting and toasting, *Rome Precincts* also sheds light on the capital's cultural highlights, from must-see ruins, basilicas and museums, to unexpected street-art murals. So mix yourself a spritz, kick back and let the following pages spark your own love affair with Italy's great protagonist.

Cristian Bonetto

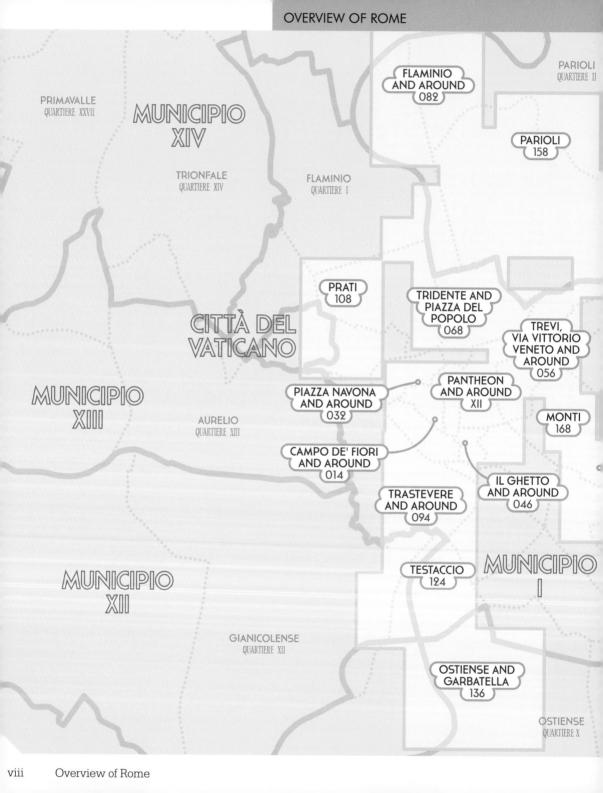

PRIMAVALLE
QUARTIERE XXVII

MUNICIPIO
XIV

TRIONFALE
QUARTIERE XIV

FLAMINIO
QUARTIERE I

FLAMINIO
AND AROUND
082

PARIOLI
QUARTIERE II

PARIOLI
158

PRATI
108

CITTÀ DEL
VATICANO

TRIDENTE AND
PIAZZA DEL
POPOLO
068

TREVI,
VIA VITTORIO
VENETO AND
AROUND
056

MUNICIPIO
XIII

AURELIO
QUARTIERE XIII

PIAZZA NAVONA
AND AROUND
032

PANTHEON
AND AROUND
XII

MONTI
168

CAMPO DE' FIORI
AND AROUND
014

IL GHETTO
AND AROUND
046

TRASTEVERE
AND AROUND
094

MUNICIPIO
XII

GIANICOLENSE
QUARTIERE XII

TESTACCIO
124

MUNICIPIO
I

OSTIENSE AND
GARBATELLA
136

OSTIENSE
QUARTIERE X

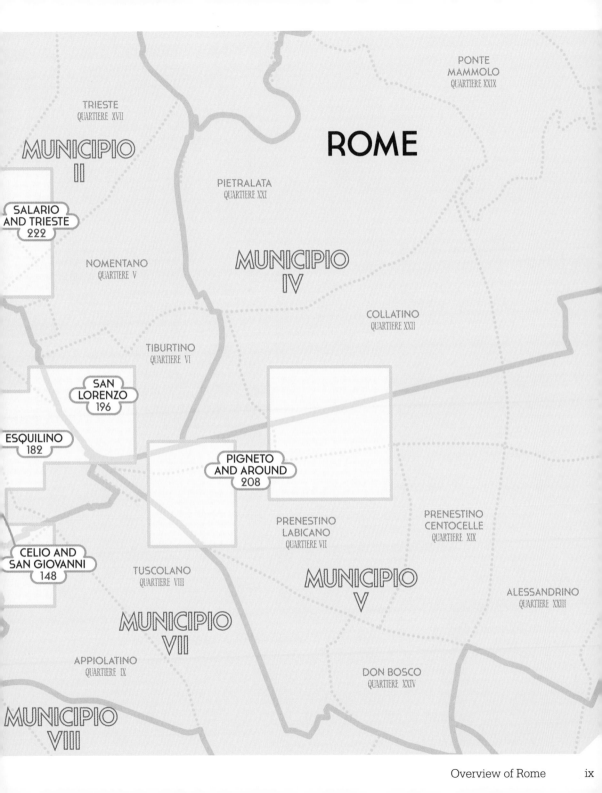

ROME

PONTE
MAMMOLO
QUARTIERE XXIX

TRIESTE
QUARTIERE XVII

MUNICIPIO
II

PIETRALATA
QUARTIERE XXI

SALARIO
AND TRIESTE
222

MUNICIPIO
IV

NOMENTANO
QUARTIERE V

COLLATINO
QUARTIERE XXII

TIBURTINO
QUARTIERE VI

SAN
LORENZO
196

ESQUILINO
182

PIGNETO
AND AROUND
208

PRENESTINO
LABICANO
QUARTIERE VII

PRENESTINO
CENTOCELLE
QUARTIERE XIX

CELIO AND
SAN GIOVANNI
148

TUSCOLANO
QUARTIERE VIII

MUNICIPIO
V

ALESSANDRINO
QUARTIERE XXIII

MUNICIPIO
VII

APPIOLATINO
QUARTIERE IX

DON BOSCO
QUARTIERE XXIV

MUNICIPIO
VIII

A PERFECT DAY IN ROME

A perfect day in Rome should start on a sweet note, so grab a take-away slice of crostata di viscole (sour cherry and ricotta tart) at **Pasticceria Boccione** (*see* p. 052) in the atmospheric Ghetto. Check out the neighbourhood's Renaissance-era **Fontana delle Tartarughe** (Fountain of the Turtles; *see* p. 055) before dropping into minimalist shop **Stay** (*see* p. 048) for contemporary Italian linen. Cross Via Arenula and slip onto Via dei Barbieri to muse over avant-garde threads, art and frescoes at concept store and gallery **Contemporary Cluster** (*see* p. 022). If you're craving coffee, slurp a good one at nearby **Roscioli Caffè Pasticceria** (*see* p. 026), making a mental note to head back one evening for cocktails in the back bar.

Once caffeinated, stroll up Via dei Giubbonari to picture-perfect **Campo de' Fiori** (*see* p. 030) and its daily market. Take notes from the local signore (women) as they eye up produce the way *Vogue* fashion editor Anna Wintour scans a runway. Take time to appreciate the Michelangelo-designed facade of **Palazzo Farnese** (*see* p. 030) on nearby Piazza Farnese before wandering down Via Monserrato, home to designer Gloria Gobbi and her upcycled kimono creations at **Antichi Kimono** (*see* p. 018). Make a hairpin turn into Via del Pellegrino to meet French expat Alain Georges at his petite retro design shop **Alain Rome** (*see* p. 016). Men itching for a Roman makeover should drop into edgy fashion store **SBU (Strategic Business Unit)** (*see* p. 034), just north of Corso Vittorio Emanuele. A block away is Rome's most celebrated square, **Piazza Navona** (*see* p. 044), home to Gian Lorenzo Bernini's epic **Fontana dei Quattro Fiumi** (Fountain of the Four Rivers; *see* p. 044). Fawn over smaller Roman wonders at contemporary jewellery showroom **Co.Ro. Jewels** (*see* p. 002) before savouring modern Roman creativity at eatery **Retrobottega** (*see* p. 007).

Drink a post-prandial espresso at classic coffee bar **Tazza d'Oro** (*see* p. 008) before arriving at Piazza della Rotonda, home to the ancient **Pantheon** (*see* p. 012). Just to the east, Rococo architecture awaits in **Piazza di Sant'Ignazio** (*see* p. 012), while 2nd-century temple ruins loom over nearby **Piazza di Pietra**. From the latter, head north into petite Via dei Bergamaschi to eye harder-to-find women's labels and accessories at **Spazioespanso** (*see* p. 004). The street spills into Piazza Colonna, home to bureaucrats, politicians and the 2nd-century **Colonna di Marco Aurelio** (*see* p. 013), carved with ancient battle scenes. Across Via del Corso awaits the stained-glass elegance of **Galleria Alberto Sordi** (*see* p. 066), a worthy pit stop on your way to Baroque showstopper **Fontana di Trevi** (Trevi Fountain; *see* p. 066). Toss a coin to guarantee your return, then stop by **Il Gelato di San Crispino** (*see* p. 061) for sublime ice-cream.

Refreshed, catch a taxi from nearby Largo del Tritone and head north to the **Museo e Galleria Borghese** (*see* p. 230), home to Cardinal Scipione Borghese's enviable cultural horde (tickets must be pre-booked online). One of Italy's most prized art collections, its pieces include Bernini's hypnotic sculpture *Ratto di Proserpina* (Rape of Proserpina) and major works by Caravaggio, Raphael and Canova. Swap soul-stirring art for views at luxe rooftop bar **Il Giardino** (*see* p. 064), atop the refreshed Hotel Eden. A flawless martini in hand, watch the sun set over the city before heading to your reserved table at legendary **Colline Emiliane** (*see* p. 058), a family-run restaurant famed for impeccable Emilian cuisine. If the night is still young, hop into a taxi and cross the Tiber for drinks in free-spirited Trastevere, toasting to la dolce vita (the sweet life) with a well-chosen vino (wine) at local favourite **Enoteca Ferrara** (*see* p. 105).

Power, both ancient and modern, reverberates on the deep streets pressed between Via del Corso and Corso del Rinascimento. Opulent palazzi (large buildings) house the country's Senate, Chamber of Deputies and prime minister, and guard the cultural riches of Rome's aristocratic families. Ecclesiastical boutiques draw preened priests to Via dei Cestari, which leads to the 2nd-century Pantheon, its piazza a sea of star-struck tourists, harried business types and the odd horse and carriage.

And while the narrow surrounding streets aren't short of tacky souvenirs and laminated menus, they also harbour a string of standout restaurants, bars, boutiques and ateliers.

Fiume Tevere

LUNGOTEVERE TOR DI NONA

VIA DELL'ORSO

Museo Napoleonico di Roma

VIA GIUSEPPE ZANARDELLI

VIA DEI SOLDATI

Museo Nazionale Romano

Piazza Lancellotti

PALAZZO ALTEMPS

VIA DELLA MASCHERA D'ORO

Piazza Fiammetta

Hotel Genio

Piazza di Sant' Apollinare

VIA DEI CORONARI

Antica Dimora delle Cinque Lune

CHIOSTRO DEL BRAMANTE

Largo Febo

L'Arciliuto (theatre)

Raphael Hotel

CHIESA DI SANTA MARIA DELLA PACE

FONTANA DEL NETTUNO

Piazza Navona

24   JUN 8OT6

SHOP
1 Co.Ro. Jewels
2 Federico Polidori
3 Spazioespanso

SHOP AND EAT
4 Confetteria Moriondo & Gariglio

PANTHEON AND AROUND

EAT
5 La Ciambella
6 Retrobottega
DRINK
7 Tazza d'Oro
8 Salotto 42
9 Sant'Eustachio Il Caffè

RETROBOTTEGA

COLONNA
RIONE III

CO.RO.
JEWELS

MUNICIPIO I

PALAZZO
CHIGI

COLONNA
DI MARCO
AURELIO

Colonna Suite
del Corso

CITTÀ DEL SOLE

SPAZIOESPANSO

SALOTTO 42

COLLEGIO

CHIESA DI
SAN LUIGI
DEI FRANCESI

GELATO
DI SAN
CRISPINO

TAZZA
D'ORO

TEMPIO DI
ADRIANO

SANT'
EUSTACHIO
RIONE VIII

ARMANDO AL
PANTHEON

CASALI

SANT'EUSTACHIO
IL CAFFÈ

L'ELEFANTINO

CONFETTERIA
MORIONDO
& GARIGLIO

FEDERICO
POLIDORI

LA CIAMBELLA

PIGNA
RIONE IX

001

1.

CO.RO. JEWELS

Via della Scrofa 52
06 4893 0454
www.corojewels.com
Open Mon–Sat 10.30am–7.30pm

Gracious young designers Costanza De Cecco and Giulia Giannini have an enviable knack for producing high-end jewellery that's equally elegant and edgy. A shared architectural background drives much of their work, with some pieces inspired by Rome's own urban landmarks. The cube-shaped Colosseo Quadrato ring takes its cue from Palazzo della Civiltà del Lavoro (dubbed the 'Square Colosseum'), while their Gasometro series of rings, cuffs, chokers, pendants and cufflinks find their muse in an old gasometer in the city's Ostiense district. Other works offer modern twists on classics, such as minimalist sculptural rings with square, semi-open bands punctuated by a single spherical gemstone. Each item is made by Tuscan artisans using gold, sterling silver, bronze and ruthenium. Prices are reasonable considering quality and uniqueness, with earrings starting from €65 and rings priced between €100 and €200. Co.Ro. is an acronym for Piazza del Collegio Romano, location of the high school where the design duo met and forged their friendship.

LOCAL TIP
For imaginative toys that inspire creativity in kids and tweens, drop by Città del Sole (Via della Scrofa 65), one of Rome's finest toyshops.

FEDERICO POLIDORI

Via del Piè di Marmo 7–8
338 7329002
www.federicopolidori.com
Open Mon–Sat 9am–12pm &
12.30–7pm

He may look a little like actor Robert De Niro, but Federico Polidori's talent lies firmly in leatherworking. The self-taught master was inspired by his nonno (grandfather), who crafted riding gear for the butteri (traditional cowboys) of southern Tuscany and northern Lazio. It's a passion that saw Federico open his own workshop in 1979, a space in which he produces finely crafted leather goods today. Drop by and you'll find him working at his huge wooden table laden with vegetable-tanned Tuscan hides and the odd Western novel (his childhood fascination with the Wild West has never abated). Off-the-shelf items include super-slim hand-stitched wallets, belts and bags, some of the latter featuring his distinctive pelle intrecciata (woven leather). Online you'll find a greater selection of bags, which Federico can make to order; waiting time for a custom-made bag is around two to three months (international shipping available). Prices start at around €180 for wallets and range from €250 to €5000 for bags.

3.

SPAZIOESPANSO

Via dei Bergamaschi 59–60
06 9784 2793
http://spazioespanso.business.site
Open Mon 2.30–7.30pm,
Tues–Sat 10.30am–7.30pm

- -

Graced with plush sofas,
candles, a grand piano and a
back garden, Spazioespanso
feels more like a luxe retreat
than a women's boutique.
But then 'ordinary' isn't in
the vocabulary of its owners,
Anna Maria Montani and
Alberto Volpe. The couple has
created one of Rome's most
seductive stores, its racks
and shelves a showcase for
highly original, harder-to-
find labels such as France's
Marc Le Bihan, Portugal's
TM Collection and Japan's
Zucca. There are only a few of
each piece, and some items
are made exclusively for the
store. The sharp curation
extends to accessories, from
artisan jewellery, millinery
and fragrances, to one-of-a-
kind bags that, for instance,
pair leather with aluminium
to extraordinary effect. You
may even score a pair of
avant-garde kicks. It's hard
to miss the giant driftwood
centrepiece, salvaged from
the coast and now one of the
city's most out-of-the-box
display settings.

4.

**CONFETTERIA
MORIONDO & GARIGLIO**

Via del Piè di Marmo 21–22
06 699 0856
http://moriondoegariglio.com
Open Mon–Sun 9am–7.30pm

- -

The great Roman poet
Trilussa was so enamoured
with Confetteria Moriondo &
Gariglio that he mentioned
it in his verses. This is
Rome's oldest purveyor of
sweet treats, established
in Turin in 1870 by the
confectioners to the royal
house of Savoy. The business
moved south to Rome in
the early 1900s, where it
has seduced tastebuds and
compromised waistlines
ever since. The irresistible
truffles and pralines are still
handmade to 19th-century
recipes, using only cocoa
butter and no preservatives.
Hazelnut lovers shouldn't
miss the signature Stella
Oro, a milk-chocolate
praline filled with hazelnut
and gianduja (chocolate
and hazelnut spread) that
pre-dates the ubiquitous
Baci Perugina. If you need
to warm up (or want a jolt),
devour a pizzutello con
grappa, a dark-chocolate
truffle filled with fiery grappa.
Other treats include pretty
fruit jellies and, at Easter,
ridiculously cute agnelli di
marzapane (marzipan lambs).
You can even order your own
chocolate 'business cards'
(order in the morning to
collect the following day).

4.

4.

3.

3.

3.

4.

5.

LA CIAMBELLA

Via dell'Arco della Ciambella 20
06 683 2930
www.la-ciambella.it
Open Tues–Sun 8am–12am

Breaking news: it is possible to eat well and among locals just two blocks from the Pantheon. Airy, modern La Ciambella is the passion project of Roman chef Francesca Ciucci and Bolognese sommelier Mirka Guberti. Together they've created an all-day bistro championing seasonal produce such as prized free-range rabbit from the Tuscia region of northern Lazio. Francesca chooses much of the produce herself and old family recipes guide the Roman-centric menu. Top picks include the strikingly yellow pasta alla carbonara or, for breakfast, the ciambellone (Italian ring cake). Mirka's passion for vino shines through in the Italo-Franco wine list, which includes small, innovative winemakers. For an intimate experience, request the private dining room, an oval-shaped hide-out for two to six guests, crowned by Mirka's grandmother's chandelier. Wherever you sit, check out the glass floor panel near the front bar: the ruins below belong to the ancient Baths of Agrippa, the first of the great thermae built in Rome.

RETROBOTTEGA
Via della Stelletta 4
06 6813 6310
www.retro-bottega.com
Open Mon 7–11.30pm,
Tues–Sun 12–11.30pm

- -

Rising culinary stars
Giuseppe Lo Iudice and
Alessandro Miocchi earned
their stripes working in the
high-pressure kitchens of
London, New York, Berlin
and northern Italy before
launching their own maverick
eatery. Much of the action
happens at two communal
oak tables, where diners
ooh, ahh and photograph
beautiful, polished creations
such as delicate tortellini
with broccoli cream, salsiccia
(sausage) and liquorice
powder. While the kitchen's
technical competency is
obvious, it's balanced by a
very Italian reverence for
simplicity and high-quality
ingredients. Both Giuseppe
and Alessandro get a kick
out of sourcing smaller Italian
producers, whose vegetables
and meats steer the monthly
changing menu. Much
of what's served is made
from scratch, including the
pasta and breads. Culinary
brilliance aside, Retrobottega
gets bonus points for
the professionalism and
friendliness of its waitstaff.
Reservations are only taken
for the degustation menu,
so if you're dining à la carte,
head in early to avoid a wait
(by 8pm for dinner).

7.

TAZZA D'ORO

Via degli Orfani 84
06 678 9792
www.tazzadorocoffeeshop.com
Mon–Sat 7am–8pm, Sun
10.30am–7.15pm

Given the quality of its coffee and proximity to the Pantheon, it's not surprising that this is Rome's busiest espresso bar. Grinding and brewing since 1946, it's as popular with local business types, shopkeepers and residents as it is with Instagramming tourists. The espresso is smooth, full-bodied and intense, though the star turn here is the refreshing granita di caffè, a lightly sweetened, blended iced coffee served con panna (with cream). Caffeine aside, I love this space for its allegorical paintings depicting the history and culture of coffee. They're deliciously retro, just like the Mid-Century signage on the exterior. The take-home coffee beans and blends make for cool souvenirs, with a nifty coffee-bean bancomat (ATM) available on the street for after-hours purchases.

LOCAL TIP
Despite its proximity to the tourist-swamped Pantheon, Armando al Pantheon (Salita dei Crescenzi 31) is a classic Roman restaurant revered by locals (reservations essential).

caffè
TAZZA
D'ORO
EL MEJOR DEL MUNDO

8.

SALOTTO 42

Piazza di Pietra 42
06 678 5804
www.salotto42.it
Open Mon–Sun 10.30am–2am

Petite Salotto 42 has it made: not only does it flank one of the city's most beautiful squares, it faces the imposing ancient columns of the Temple of Hadrian. In the warmer months, a table under the bougainvillea is the best seat in the house. The lounge bar itself is a retreat to ensconce yourself in; it's speckled with vintage furniture, coffee-table books on art, design and fashion, and an international crowd. There's a decent selection of teas, plus the usual spirited suspects, from Aperol spritzes and slinky martinis to Moscow mules concocted with house-made ginger beer. While the venue is open all day, it's at its most alluring in the late afternoon or evening. Cin cin!

9.

SANT'EUSTACHIO IL CAFFÈ

Piazza Sant'Eustachio 82
06 6880 2048
www.santeustachioilcaffe.it
Open Sun–Thurs 7.30am–1am,
Fri 7.30am–1.30am,
Sat 7.30am–2am

Like its rival Tazza d'Oro (*see* p. 008), retro espresso bar and coffee roaster Sant'Eustachio is cult-status material. Kicking since 1938, it retains its original mosaic floor and furnishings, while the scattering of outdoor tables is perfect for a caffeine fix with a side of people-watching. It's a popular haunt for politici (politicians), who fuel up before a day of infighting at the nearby Senate. The espresso here is famous for its rich, thick crema, made by adding a few drops of espresso to sugar and beating it into a frothy paste before pouring the rest of the coffee. If you prefer unsweetened, request it amaro (without sugar) at the counter. For a decadent alternative, order the mousse al caffè, a velvety concoction made with espresso, eggs, whipped cream and sugar, or the monachella, an espresso with chocolate and whipped cream. Whatever you choose, put a spring in your step with a side of chicchi di caffè (coffee beans dipped in dark chocolate).

8.

salotto.42

LOCAL TIP
Via degli Orfani leads
north-east from the
Pantheon to pretty Piazza
Capranica and Collegio
(Piazza Capranica 99),
a fashionable bar-
restaurant that pours
delectable cocktails.

9.

Torrefazione Artigianale a Legna

SCIENZA E CAFFÈ

METODI
DI PREPARAZIONE
DEL CAF

Sant'Eustachio®   il caffè
dal 1938 a Roma

LA CIMBALI

stre Specialità fredde

| Caffè freddo | Frappè | Shakerato | Romeo e Giulietta |
| con panna | | | |

a, con caffè equo e solidale, biologico, tostato a legna

The district is anchored by the mighty **Pantheon** (Piazza della Rotonda), one of the oldest and most architecturally influential buildings in the Western world. Commissioned by the emperor Hadrian and dating from around 125 CE, its 16 Corinthian columns were carved from a single block of Egyptian granite. A testament to Roman engineering, the building's unreinforced concrete dome remains the largest of its kind in the world, nearly 2000 years since its creation. From Piazza della Rotonda, Via Giustiniani leads west to the Baroque **Chiesa di San Luigi dei Francesi** (Piazza di San Luigi dei Francesi), famed for its *St Matthew Cycle*, a trio of paintings by Caravaggio. The church itself has served Rome's French community since 1589.

East of Piazza della Rotonda, razor-thin Via del Seminario leads to theatrical **Piazza di Sant'Ignazio di Loyola**, a Rococo square reminiscent of a stage set. Pop into the square's 17th-century **Chiesa di Sant'Ignazio di Loyola** to eye up its deceptive 'dome' – in reality a clever trompe l'oeil fresco by Andrea Pozzo.

Right behind the Pantheon is the **Elefantino** (Piazza della Minerva), a criminally cute statue of an elephant carrying a 6th-century BCE Egyptian obelisk on its back. Designed by Gian Lorenzo Bernini, it dates from 1667. Say 'ciao', then slip into the square's **Basilica di Santa Maria Sopra Minerva**, a 13th-century Gothic church guilty of a few nips and tucks. Its highlights include 15th-century frescoes by Renaissance artist

Filippino Lippi in the Cappella Carafa (Carafa Chapel) and a sculpture of Christ by the great Michelangelo. Christ's jarring bronze drapery was never part of the artist's original design; prudish sentiments saw it added at a later date.

For masterful brushstrokes and aristocratic interior design, make time for the sumptuous **Galleria Doria Pamphilj** (Via del Corso 305). One of Rome's top private art collections, its assets include paintings by Raphael, Caravaggio, Titian and Velázquez. The latter artist is responsible for the gallery's most celebrated canvas, a portrait of Pope Innocent X, considered by numerous art critics to be the finest portrait ever executed.

A few blocks further north, drop in on the Italian prime minister at his 16th-century city pad, **Palazzo Chigi** (Piazza Colonna 370). One-hour guided tours – which run twice monthly on Saturday mornings from September to June – should be booked in advance; see http://governo.it for details. Punctuating Piazza Colonna itself is the **Colonna di Marco Aurelio**, a less than humble 2nd-century column depicting Roman emperor Marcus Aurelius' military victories.

The area bordered by Corso Vittorio Emanuele II, Via Arenula and the River Tiber is anchored by the poetically named Campo de' Fiori (Field of Flowers), a photogenic square famed for its appetite-piquing market stalls and late-night revelry.

Beyond it, history-steeped cobbled streets Via del Pellegrino and Via di Monserrato house a sophisticated mix of antique stores, independent fashion boutiques, cafes and restaurants. The area's architectural wonders include some of the city's finest Renaissance palazzi (large buildings). Top billing goes to Palazzo Farnese, partly designed by Michelangelo and dressed in frescoes that give the Sistine Chapel stiff competition.

24   JUN 8076

SHOP
1 ALAIN ROME
2 IBIZ
3 ANTICHI KIMONO
4 GALLERIA VARSI
5 GROOVE ROME BERLIN
6 ONEROOM

SHOP AND DRINK
7 CONTEMPORARY CLUSTER

17

EAT
8 PIANOSTRADA
9 SUPPLIZIO
10 FATAMORGANA

EAT AND DRINK
11 ROSCIOLI CAFFÈ PASTICCERIA
12 BARNUM CAFÉ

DRINK
13 IL GOCCETTO

CAMPO DE' FIORI AND AROUND

La Suite
del Barone

LA GRANDE BELLEZZA

⊕ FONTANA DEI QUATTRO FIUMI

CHIESA DI
SANT' AGNESE
IN AGONE

Piazza
Navona

OFFICINA PROFUMO
FARMACEUTICA DI
SANTA MARIA NOVELLA

FONTANA
DEL MORO

0   50 m

N

PARIONE
RIONE VI

Piazza di
Pasquino

Museo
di Roma

San
Pantaleo

Hotel
Navona

Piazza dei
Caprettari

CORSO VITTORIO EMANUELE II

**BARNUM
CAFÉ** TINA
SONDERGAARD

**BASILICA DI
SAN LORENZO
IN DAMASO**

Museo
di Scultura Antica
Giovanni Barracco

Largo del
Teatro
Valle

← **ALAIN
ROME**

TO SUPPLIZIO
& IL GOCCETTO
(SEE MAP LEFT)

Mostra
Leonardo
da Vinci

PALAZZO
DELLA
CANCELLERIA

CORSO VITTORIO EMANUELE II

HOSTARIA
COSTANZA

Basilica di
Sant'Andrea
della Valle

Piazza
Vidoni

Hotel
Tiziano

**ANTICHI
KIMONO**

FORNO
CAMPO
DE'FIORI

Casa di
Santa
Brigida

Exe Hotel
dellaTorre
Argentina

Mercato
di Campo
de' Fiori

Farnese
(cinema)

**GALLERIA
VARSI**

**CONTEMPORARY
CLUSTER**

Piazza del
Biscione

ONEROOM

**SANT'
EUSTACHIO**
RIONE VIII

Piazza
Farnese

**GROOVE
ROME
BERLIN**

IBIZ

FATAMORGANA

PALAZZO
FARNESE

FORNO
ROSCIOLI

Santi Biagio
e Carlo ai
Catinari

ARCO
FARNESE

Piazza del
Monte di Pietà

Fontana del
Mascherone

PALAZZO
SPADA

**ROSCIOLI
CAFFÈ
PASTICCERIA**

ARENULA/
CAIROLI

REGOLA
RIONE VII

Piazza della
Trinità dei
Pellegrini

PIANOSTRADA

Fiume Tevere

MUNICIOPIO I

Piazza
Cenci

Piazza
Trilussa

LUNGOTEVERE DELLA FARNESINA

(River Tiber)

ARENULA/
MIN. G. GIUSTIZIA

Fontana
di Ponte
Sisto

VALLATI

015

1.

ALAIN ROME

Via del Pellegrino 171
06 6880 7747
http://alainrome.com
Open Mon–Sat 10am–1.30pm
& 4–7.30pm

Seeking a Mid-Century Italian lamp? A vintage Parisian nightclub booklet? Perhaps a snake-skin African drinking flask? Chances are you'll find it in this little treasure trove, owned by Parisian expat Alain Georges and his Roman wife Alessandra Durando. Alain has great fun researching each piece, sourcing a lot of his finds in the south of France and only choosing objects that speak to him. The end result is a space in which every item comes with an interesting anecdote. I always stumble across something rare and fabulous here, whether it be a Mid-Century abstract coffee table from France, a retro '70s Italian vase or vintage travel guides. I recently fawned over a ridiculously cool set of 10 polka-dot Italian punch cups with matching bowl from the 1920s for €100. Some of Alain's most personally prized possessions are those behind his desk: politely ask if they're for sale – you may just be able to bag one.

LOCAL TIP
For impeccable cocktails and a speakeasy vibe, call ahead to book a table at the secretive Jerry Thomas Project (Vicolo Cellini 30; 370 1146287).

IBIZ

Via dei Chiavari 39
06 6830 7297
www.ibizroma.it
Open Mon–Sat 9.30am–
7.30pm

Beautiful handcrafted leather goods are the draw at this intimate workshop. Chances are you'll find artisan Elisa Nepi at her work table or on the vintage Necci sewing machine. The latter was used to sew the saddles for William Wyler's blockbuster *Ben-Hur*, filmed at Rome's Cinecittà studios. Ibiz was opened by Elisa's parents Fulvio and Simonetta almost 50 years ago, and the family-run business now also includes Elisa's sister-in-law, Flavia. Only Italian leather from Tuscany and the Veneto is used here, transformed into everything from handbags and totes to wallets, coin purses and toiletry bags. Many of the creations have playful, idiosyncratic details, whether it's a ribbon-shaped women's belt or a wallet featuring multi-coloured internal panels. Each piece is designed and produced on-site, with bags starting at less than €50, belts going for €30 to €40 and unisex toiletry bags for around €70. Best of all, products are serviced for life.

3.

ANTICHI KIMONO

Via di Monserrato 43B
06 6813 5876
www.antichikimono.com
Open Mon 3.30–7.30pm,
Tues–Sat 10.30am–2pm &
3.30–7.30pm

East and West meld to
fetching effect at Antichi
Kimono. At the helm is
talented designer Gloria
Gobbi, who transforms
vintage Japanese kimonos
and Indian saris into high-
quality one-off pieces,
including skirts, gilets
(sleeveless jackets) and
hand-stitched, richly textured
jackets. The latter retail for
around €120. The fabrics
here are a highlight, such as
silk that's been embroidered
with gold thread, or dyed
by folding, twisting and
bunching in a traditional
Japanese technique known as
shibori. In addition to Gloria's
own creations, you'll find
sculptural plissé (crinkled)
garments from France, as
well as a small selection of
handsome kimonos for male
individualists. Accessories
range from pure cashmere
scarves sourced directly from
traditional weavers in Indian
Kashmir to highly creative
Italian jewellery that may
see you don a 3D-printed
bracelet or striking earrings
made from upcycled plastic
bottles. The store also opens
on Sundays in peak periods,
most notably during the
lead-up to Christmas.

4.

GALLERIA VARSI

Via di Grotta Pinta 38
06 686 5415
http://galleriavarsi.it
Open Tues–Sat 12–8pm,
Sun 3–8pm

Topical, top-tier street art is
the focus at Galleria Varsi, a
private gallery established
by young Roman aficionado
Massimo Scrocca. Since
opening in 2013, the gallery
has exhibited some of the
world's most coveted talent,
from New York's Skeme
to Spain's Daniel Muñoz,
Australia's Fintan Magee
and home-grown shakers
such as abstract artist
Roberto Ciredz. The works
are specially commissioned
for the gallery, with around
six to seven exhibitions each
year. If your budget doesn't
permit the purchase of an
original work, the gallery
stocks limited-edition silk-
screen prints created by a
variety of artists and retailing
for around €100. You'll also
find back catalogues of
previous exhibitions (written
in English and Italian), as
well as a curated selection of
niche street-art tomes that
skip the obvious, easy-to-find
titles (no Banksy books here).
Of course, you can always
drop by simply to muse on
the exhibitions themselves,
a refreshing antidote to
the area's glut of Virgins,
saints and cherubs.

LOCAL TIP
Grotto-like Hostaria Costanza (Piazza del Paradiso 55) serves Roman cuisine among the ancient ruins of Teatro di Pompeo (reservations recommended).

3.

4.

3.

5.

GROOVE ROME BERLIN
Piazza Farnese 45
06 6880 4048
www.groovefashion.it
Open Mon–Sat 10.30am–8pm,
Sun 10.30am–2pm & 3–8pm

Facing the glorious Renaissance-era Palazzo Farnese, Groove Rome Berlin lures with its booty of affordable, quality urbanwear for men and women. Dividing his time between the Rome store and a Berlin offshoot, owner Fabrizio Astrologo gets a kick out of sourcing new local and international brands, many of which he finds at Copenhagen, Berlin and Rome fashion weeks. It's a global affair, with a mix of labels covering everything from graphic tees and soft knits, to sweaters, party frocks, jeans and outerwear. Slip into Lee denim and organic cotton threads from Italy's own Dissolved Labs, or fight indecision over a whole wall of limited edition sneakers from New Balance and Barcelona import Munich. You can score a great knit or blouse here for around €50, a pair of chinos for around €70, or a puffer coat for around €90. Accessories include socks, bags, Alkimy fragrances and sunglasses from Germany's Dress Your Mind.

ONEROOM
Piazza dei Satiri 55
338 7229120
http://oneroom.it
Open Tues–Sat 4–7pm
(or by appointment)

Oneroom is no ordinary bookshop; it's more a pocket-sized cultural salon, with two Mid-Century Italian armchairs on standby for those wanting to read or chat with kind-hearted, unassuming owner Stefano Ruffa. The shelves are dedicated to contemporary photography, which Stefano sees as a way to view life through fresh eyes; one shelf is dedicated to photography books about Rome, another to Italian photographers, but the vast majority of titles have an international focus, whether Nordic photography or travel. There's also some rare photojournalism books from the 1960s and '70s. Not all are for sale; some are simply for browsing – Stefano's way of ensuring books of great beauty are accessible to all. Oneroom also hosts photography exhibitions that explore the relationship between photography and other disciplines, from painting to science. One past exhibition, curated by Max Renkel, included works by Cy Twombly and Patti Smith.

Campo de' Fiori and around

CONTEMPORARY CLUSTER

Via dei Barbieri 7
06 6830 8388
www.contemporarycluster.com
Open Tues 11am–9pm, Wed–
Thurs 11am–11.45pm, Fri–Sat
11am–1.30am, Sun 11am–12am

Conceptualised by Rome
gallerist Giacomo Guidi
and set in a 17th-century
palazzo, Contemporary Cluster
combines contemporary art,
architecture, fashion, design
and music to impressive
effect. The ground floor
spotlights avant-garde
fashion designers like
Lumen et Umbra and Label
Under Construction, whose
statement pieces hang on
racks made from World War
I military beds. A vintage
pharmacy counter displays
niche, luxe cosmetics
and fragrances, and a bar
serves coffee, cocktails and
light bites. A staircase by
Rationalist architect Marco
Fiorentino leads to the
mezzanine, home to art,
design and travel tomes from
niche publishers, a small
selection of vinyl, and high-
end retro furniture designed
for lounging. Another flight
of stairs leads to the main
exhibition space, where
rotating contemporary shows
have included artists like
rising Lithuanian star Tadao
Cern. Don't forget to look up
at the ceiling, graced with
Baroque frescoes by Giacinto
and Ludovico Gimignani.

PIANOSTRADA

Via delle Zoccolette 22
06 8957 2296
Open Tues–Fri 1–4pm
& 7–11.30pm, Sat–Sun
10.30am–11.30pm

In only a few short years, Chiara Magliocchetti, chef Paola Colucci and Paola's daughters, Flaminia and Alice Spognetta, have turned their buzzing bistro into a verified hotspot. A seat at the kitchen bar counter is always entertaining, but the best are in the back garden, a scene seemingly pulled off the pages of *Vogue Living*. Bucolic setting aside, what I love is the flexibility of the menu, which offers quick, casual bites like focaccia with fig compote, cured ham and basil; gourmet burgers; creative cicchetti (tapas); and more elaborate dishes. Pasta options skip the clichés, with refreshing highs such as spaghettoni with fresh and oven-baked datterini tomatoes, Sardinian ricotta mustia, Parmigiano-Reggiano and zesty lemon.

I also appreciate the dedicated list of seasonal vegetable dishes like pan-fried escarole (endive) sexed up with toasted pine nuts, capers, olives and raisins. The bread is made in-house, and the herbs are picked fresh from the garden. Book ahead for dinner (or lunch on weekends).

9.

SUPPLIZIO

Via dei Banchi Vecchi 143
06 8987 1920
www.supplizioroma.it
Open Mon–Sat 11.30am–4pm
& 4.30–10pm

Top-notch wallet-friendly street food? Sì, grazie! Co-owned by renowned chef Arcangelo Dandini, this small eat-and-go turns the humble supplì (rice ball) into a culinary revelation. Each golden wonder is fried to perfection, with enviable firmness and crunch, and a soft, moist filling. Variations include cacio e pepe (pecorino romano cheese and black pepper) and pomodoro e basilico (tomato and basil). The secret is high-quality ingredients, from the Puglian olive oil to the cheeses and salumi (cured meats). And while the rice balls are the irrefutable stars, the menu delivers some other smash hits, among them polpette di tonno (tuna 'meatballs'), grilled and then lightly smoked. The panini are also a good bet, made using brioche-like buns from celebrated bakery Roscioli (*see* p. 026) and filled with combos like sgombro (mackerel), puntarelle (Catalonian chicory) and house-made mayo. Last but not least, is the obscenely sexy salty-sweet crema fritta (fried cream), made with eggs, pecorino cheese, cane sugar and cinnamon.

10.

FATAMORGANA

Via dei Chiavari 37
06 8881 8437
www.gelateriafatamorgana.com
Open Sun–Thurs 12–11pm,
Fri–Sat 12pm–12am

Gelato is serious business in Rome, and countless gelato snobs swear by Fatamorgana, domain of actor-turned-gelato-goddess Maria Agnese. Her rotating repertoire of more than 400 gluten-free flavours spans the classic to the wildly creative. Will you succumb to the toasted almond with green cardamom, the lemon curd, or the chocolate scented with tobacco leaves? Those with a truly adventurous palate can try boundary-pushing combos like the knock-out black garlic with white chocolate or bold-and-tangy Seades, fusing Sardinian pecorino cheese, chestnuts and orange peel. Servers are generous with tastings and happy to suggest suitable pairings. Expect to be blown away by the authenticity of the flavours. Only fresh, premium ingredients are used, with no fillers, fake flavours or other nasty additives. You can even grab a box set of 'sushi gelato', made to look like California rolls. So good. You'll find other outlets across the city, including in Monti, home to the original shop.

10.

10.

10.

9.

9.

9.

11.

ROSCIOLI CAFFÈ PASTICCERIA

Piazza Benedetto Cairoli 16
06 8916 5330
www.rosciolicaffe.com
Open Mon–Sat 7am–11pm,
Sun 8am–6pm

Roscioli is a byword for high-quality eats in Rome. Brothers Pierluigi and Alessandro own this slinky cafe, pastry shop and cocktail bar in one. Slip inside for rich espresso, fresh cornetti (Italian croissants), maritozzi (yeasted sweet buns filled with whipped cream) and photogenic petits fours. Panini are made with Roscioli's own prized bread. Behind the standing-room-only bar is a charcoal-hued backroom, where the cognoscenti gather at a communal table to chow from the daily menu or sip creative cocktails. Talented barkeeper Dino Boraso mixes some of the best drinks in Rome, his meticulous approach matching A-list cocktail dens in New York, London and Melbourne. Libations have included carciofo alla romana, a blend of artichoke-infused gin, maraschino, vermouth, lemon and mentuccia romana (Roman mint). The cafe's contemporary interiors are the work of Italian–Australian architects Morq, whose design plays on the idea of 'day' (the front bar) and 'night' (the back).

LOCAL TIP
For deliciously thin, crisp pizza al taglio (pizza by the slice), pop into Forno Campo de' Fiori (Campo de' Fiori 22).

BARNUM CAFÉ
Via del Pellegrino 87
06 6476 0483
www.barnumcafe.com
Open Mon–Sat 8.30am–2am

This is one of my favourite hide-outs in the centre of Rome, a cosy cafe decked out with old wooden tables, industrial lamps, and vintage liquor and circus posters. You'll find a mix of locals and tourists guzzling everything from silky cappuccinos and freshly squeezed juices, to wine and spritzes. Unlike Rome's old-school espresso bars, this is a place made for kicking back. Free wi-fi and communal tables make it a great spot to flip open your laptop after the busy lunch period, and it's a fun spot to simply people-watch. Cakes are homemade using organic eggs and usually include a few vegan options (the brownies are especially popular). If you're hankering for something savoury, scan the blackboard for the likes of soulful tagliatelle al ragù or pumpkin and ricotta tortino (tartlet) with parmesan fondue. Come Friday lunchtime, follow owner Daniele's lead and enjoy a guacapollo sandwich, a concoction of marinated chicken breast, guacamole and tomato on house-baked bread.

13.

IL GOCCETTO

Via dei Banchi Vecchi 14
06 686 4268
Open Mon 6pm–12am,
Tues–Sat 12–2.30pm &
6pm–12am

Veteran Il Goccetto isn't short of friends. Come evening, the wine bar's handful of tables quickly fill up, the rest of the crowd happily lingering by the bar or spilling out onto the postcard-pretty street, wine glasses in hand. The level of affection here is so strong that some locals have vowed to buy the well-worn wooden counter at any price should owner Anna Sbarro and her sons, Federico and Flavio, ever decide to part with it. Nostalgia is thick in the air, from the vintage Vino e Olio sign above the entrance to the old black-and-white photographs and painted 18th-century ceiling. Wrought-iron chandeliers light soaring shelves lined with around 500 mostly Italian wines, including drops from Lazio winemakers De Sanctis and Castel de Paolis. The day's wines by the glass are written on the blackboard behind the bar, and a glass cabinet tempts with tapas-style bites like marinated eggplant and grilled artichokes, buffalo mozzarella and quiche-like tielle.

Try to hit **Campo de' Fiori** in the morning, when the produce stalls are bursting with colour and volume. That hooded monk overlooking proceedings is 16th-century philosopher **Giordano Bruno**, one of many ill-fated thinkers executed right here on the square during the Roman Inquisition.

Shooting north-west from the square is Via del Pellegrino. Search out number 19, where the **Arco degli Acetari** (Vinger Makers' Arch) leads to a tiny medieval square worthy of your Instagram account. Directly across the road is the altogether more ambitious **Palazzo della Cancelleria**, accessed from Piazza della Cancelleria off Corso Vittorio Emanuele II. Designed by Renaissance architect Donato Bramante and built

between 1483 and 1513 for Cardinal Raffaele Riario, it is now home to the Holy See's highest ecclesiastical court, the Roman Rota. Its courtyard is worth a peek for the elegant double loggia. The complex also incorporates the 4th-century **Basilica di San Lorenzo in Damaso**, one of the city's oldest churches.

Bramante's assistant, Antonio da Sangallo the Younger, was the original talent behind the **Palazzo Farnese** (Piazza Farnese), located a short walk south of the Basilica di San Lorenzo in Damaso. The palazzo's current facade is credited to Michelangelo. Guided tours of the building run on Monday, Wednesday and Friday afternoons and take in spectacular frescoes by Annibale and Agostino Carracci. Tours last 45 minutes and must be booked at least one week in advance; head to www.inventerrome.com for details. Upcycling of the ancient kind is evident in Piazza Farnese's twin **fountains**, their granite baths carted in from Rome's once-lavish Terme di Caracalla.

For more Renaissance Rome, wander further south to Via Giulia, a long, cobbled street designed by Bramante and punctuated by Michelangelo's **Arco Farnese** (Farnese Arch).

From Piazza Farnese, Vicolo dei Venti leads south-east to **Palazzo Spada** (Piazza Capo di Ferro 13), a Mannerist palace famed for its forced perspective colonnade. Designed by Baroque architect Francesco Borromini, the corridor appears much longer than its actual 9-metre length. The secret is its gradually rising floor, descending ceiling and diminishing

row of columns. Upstairs, the palace houses a compact collection of 16th- and 17th-century artworks from greats including Titian, Guido Reni, Guercino and Artemisia Gentileschi. Cinephiles take note: several scenes from Paolo Sorrentini's Oscar-winning 2013 film *La grande bellezza* (The Great Beauty) were shot here.

Piazza di San Salvatore in Lauro

VIA DEI VECCHIARELLI

Piazza dei Coronari

VIA DEI CORONARI

VIA DI PANICO

CASALI

VICOLO DOMIZIO

TO MAP RIGHT (ALONG VIA DEI CORONARI)

VICOLO DELLA CAMPANELLA

VICOLO

VIA DI MONTE GIORDANO

VICOLO DI SAN GIULIANO

GIULIO PASSAMI L'OLIO

VIA DEGLI ORSINI

VIA DEI BANCHI NUOVI

Roughly framed by Corso del Rinascimento, Corso Vittorio Emanuele II and the River Tiber, this corner of Rome's centro storico (historic centre) claims the city's most celebrated square, Piazza Navona. Its sweep of Baroque palazzi (large buildings) and exuberant fountains lure everyone from spritz-sipping out-of-towners to street artists and the odd Hollywood film crew (you may recall Matt Damon and Cate Blanchett crossing the piazza in *The Talented Mr Ripley*).

The soulful tangle of streets include to the west Via dei Coronari, flanked by antiques vendors, upmarket galleries and one-off boutiques, and to the south Via del Governo Vecchio, pimped with hopping bars and eateries.

24   JUN 8OT6

SHOP
1 SBU (Strategic Business Unit)
2 Casali
3 Essenzialmente Laura
4 Privè Concept

SHOP AND EAT
5 Libera + Soon

EAT
6 Coromandel
7 Giulio Passami L'Olio

DRINK
8 Etablì
9 G-Bar
10 Caffetteria Chiostro del Bramante

PIAZZA NAVONA AND AROUND

Chiesa di
San Salvatore
in Lauro

PRIVÈ
CONCEPT

VIA   DEI   CORONARI

TO
CASALI &
GUILIO PASSAMI L'OLIO
(SEE MAP LEFT)

←

ESSENZIALMENTE
LAURA

VIA DELLA MASCHERA   D'ORO
Piazza
Fiammetta

Hotel
Genio

VIA   DEI   TRE   ARCHI

Antica Dimora
delle Cinque
Lune

VIA   DEI   CORONARI

VICOLO DI MONTEVECCHIO

ARCO

VICOLO DI FEBO

Largo
Febo

PONTE
RIONE V

VIA DELLA VETRINA

VICOLO DELLE

L'Arciliuto
(theatre)

Piazza di
Montevecchio

CHIOSTRO
DEL BRAMANTE

DELLA

ORSI

DEGLI

PACE

CAFFETTERIA
CHIOSTRO DEL
BRAMANTE

Raphael
Hotel

COROMANDEL

ETABLÌ

VACCHE

VICOLO DEL FICO

Piazza
del Fico

VIA DELLA PACE

VICOLO

VIA DELLA PACE

CHIESA DI
SANTA MARIA
DELLA PACE

Chiesa di
Santa Maria
dell'Anima

VIA DI SANTA MARIA DELL'ANIMA

La Suite
del Barone

VIA DEL CORALLO

VIA DELLA

FOSSA

VIA DI TOR   MILLINA

TO
PIAZZA
NAVONA
→

LA GRANDE
BELLEZZA

MUNICIPIO I

PARIONE

VIA DEL

0   50 m

VIA

Chiesa di
San Tommaso
in Parione

VIA DI

LIBERA +
SOON

VICOLO   DE   CUPIS

CHIESA DI
SANT' AGNESE
IN AGONE

VIA DI SANTA MARIA DELL'ANIMA

PARIONE
RIONE VI

VICOLO DEL GOVERNO VECCHIO

GOVERNO   VECCHIO

VIA DEL TEATRO PACE

VICOLO   DEI   GRANARI

Natività di
Nostro Signore
Gesù Cristo

VIA DEL   GOVERNO   VECCHIO

Chiesa della
Natività di
Gesù

VIA SORA

VICOLO DELLA CANCELLERIA

SAVELLI

N

Piazza di Pasquino

VIA

CORSO   VITTORIO   EMANUELE II

G-BAR

SBU
(STRATEGIC BUSINESS UNIT)

033

1.

SBU (STRATEGIC BUSINESS UNIT)
Via di San Pantaleo 68–69
06 6880 2547
www.sbu.it
Open Mon–Sat 10am–7.30pm,
Sun 12–7pm

SBU is a hit with everyone from young architects to rock stars. The star label is SBU itself, created by siblings Cristiano and Patrizio Perfetti and best defined as understated Italian style meets Nordic minimalism. The range includes sartorially detailed shirts, thin-knit jumpers, tweaked takes on the field jacket, as well as versatile stretch-wool jackets. SBU's coveted jeans (around €180 to €200) are made using high-grade Japanese denim, with around 10 models on offer. Chinos and corduroy pants are also available, as well as simple tees, leather jackets and a range of slimline suits (around €670). Suit alterations take around two days, and bespoke suits can be made on request and take around four weeks to complete (worldwide delivery available). Accessories include a fetching selection of mostly Italian shoes and boots, belts, cufflinks, baseball caps, briefs and backpacks. The space is gorgeous, clad in timber floorboards from old cargo trains and fitted with vintage shelves and cabinets.

LOCAL TIP
Shop for historic fragrances and toiletries at Officina Profumo Farmaceutica di Santa Maria Novella (Corso del Rinascimento 47), established in Florence in 1612.

CASALI
Via dei Coronari 115
06 687 3705
www.casali.com
Open Mon–Fri 10am–1pm &
3–7.30pm, Sat 10am–1pm

Bare walls yearn for Casali, one of Rome's finest purveyors of original and reproduction prints and etchings. Run by the Casali family since 1878, the shop is a treasure trove of vintage wonders, both large and small. You'll find 19th-century depictions of Rome, fantastical scenes from mythology, as well as hypnotic 18th-century maps detailing anything from winds and monsoons to steamy Southeast Asia. Connoisseurs go giddy over the original Piranesi etchings, among them owner Alessandra Casali, who loves nothing more than showing off the store's rarities, many of which lurk in wooden drawers. Casali's own reproduction prints are gorgeous, printed in black and white and then individually hand-painted for a more nuanced, authentic result. You can pick up a small 19th-century item here for less than €20, making it a great place for a unique local gift. There's a second branch on Piazza Navona, run by Alessandra's mother, Silvia, and brother Claudio.

3.

ESSENZIALMENTE LAURA

Via dei Coronari 57
06 686 4224
www.essenzialmentelaura.it
Open Mon–Sun
10.30am–7.30pm

Laura Bosetti Tonnato has no ordinary nose. The perfumer extraordinaire has created bespoke fragrances for Queen Elizabeth II and Russia's Hermitage Museum, and landed her an Order of Merit of the Italian Republic. In her apothecary-like store, the 'Essenzialmente Laura' line of fragrances is made with top-quality, often rare ingredients, among them the Taif rose, an oil-rich 30-petal damask rose found in Saudi Arabia. You'll find perfumes with top-note combinations like oud and sandalwood, violet and mandarin leaves, and opoponax (sweet myrrh) and musk, spanning the light and floral to the heady and leathery. A 100 millilitre bottle of eau de parfum is priced under €100. The body lotions and shower gel are superb, too, as are the scented candles and home fragrances. Laura also showcases a small rotating selection of objects by other Italian artisans, from jewellery to bags. Even the gift wrap is arresting, depicting Mary Magdalene – patron saint of perfume makers.

PRIVÈ CONCEPT
Via dei Coronari 192
366 4474247
www.priveconcept.it
Open Mon 3.30–7.30pm,
Tues–Sun 11am–7.30pm

Diddì and Giovanna will make you feel like you're playing dress-ups in their quirky, pocket-sized boutique. This is a place for female individualists, with an eclectic mix of clothing and accessories from lesser-known labels such as Treviso's Momonì, Florence's Pink Memories and Puglia's Nineminutes. Raid the racks and you might stumble upon distressed Levis 501s with eco-leather gold side stripes, a puff-sleeve sweatshirt energised with a bold embroidered back panel, or any number of idiosyncratic wearables from emerging designers. Accessories are equally creative, whether it's handmade jewellery made from ecclesiastical fabrics, sparkly socks, or handmade hats from Florentine milliner Cristina e i suoi colori (Cristina and her colours). You're also likely to find pieces by Florentine Bottega di Sguardi, famed for tinted eyewear. The palpable Tuscan presence is no coincidence; both Diddì and Giovanna hail from Lazio's northern neighbour.

5.

LIBERA + SOON

Via del Teatro Pace 41
06 6880 3363
Open Mon–Tue 9am–9pm,
Wed–Sun 9am–11pm

While tourists get hassled by touts a street away, those in the know sip, sup and browse at this tranquil oasis of civility and style. A cafe and concept store in one, it's a soothing spot for cake and coffee (served in vintage porcelain cups), light lunch fare such as quiche and salad, or an aperitivo enjoyed mostly with locals. The store takes up the back half of the space, where you might discover anything (and everything) from bright Italian ceramics and vintage English porcelain, to designer Dutch lamps, French–Tunisian throws and artisanal Puglian pasta. It's an eclectic collection of finds guided by owner Elisabetta Remondi's personal taste. If she doesn't like it, she won't sell it. The space also hosts photography exhibitions, including the work of non-professionals. According to Elisabetta, the amateur shots are sometimes the most engaging and revealing.

6.

COROMANDEL

Via di Monte Giordano 60–61
06 6880 2461
www.coromandel.it
Open Tues–Sat 8.30am–3pm
& 8–11pm, Sun 8.30am–6pm

Individualist Katia Minniti wanted a warm, enveloping space for her all-day cafe-restaurant. The result is this emerald-hued hideaway, a whimsical mishmash of vintage stage-set models, tarot-card tabletops and flea-market furniture. In the kitchen, Ornella De Felice cooks up proper brunch dishes such as French toast, eggs Benedict and croissants, a short lunch menu of seasonal comfort food, and fabulously creative fare in the evenings – think creamed baccalà (salted cod) with smoked paprika, tabasco and spicy 'nduja (spreadable Calabrian salami) in a crunchy cannolo shell. The undisputed smash is the spaghettone, an intense and complex pasta dish with shrimp crudo and lime-and-rum mojito that never fails to knock me for six. Produce is paramount, with organic meats from master butcher Roberto Liberati, seafood from lauded fishmonger Anticha Pescheria Galluzzi, and breads made in-house using organic, stone-ground flour. Best of all, service is refreshingly personable yet professional, whether you're dining solo or in company.

5.

6.

7.

GIULIO PASSAMI L'OLIO
Via di Monte Giordano 28
06 6880 3288
www.giuliopassamilolio.it
Open Mon–Sun 12–2.30pm &
7.30–11.30pm

The sign on the vintage doorway reads *Attenti al padrone. È pazzo* (Beware of the owner. He's crazy). Relax. Riccardo is a larger-than-life local personality, holding court with his made-for-radio voice and this much-loved Roman restaurant. It's an eclectic setting of old paintings, vintage erotic photographs and random ephemera, best experienced in the evening when candles light up a cosy, convivial scene of locals and out-of-towners. The menu itself delivers straightforward home cooking, from classic appetisers such as prosciutto and mozzarella to Roman pasta staples like tonnarelli all'amatriciana (pasta with tomato sauce, pecorino romano cheese and guanciale – cured pig's cheek). One truly exceptional dish is the tortellini in brodo (tortellini pasta in broth). Served in the cooler months, it's one of the finest versions I've ever slurped south of Bologna. While most dishes won't knock your culinary socks off, you can expect a tasty, satisfying feed in one of the area's most atmospheric eateries. Book ahead for dinner.

ETABLÌ

Vicolo delle Vacche 9
06 9761 6694
www.etabli.it
Open Mon–Wed 7am–1am,
Thurs–Sat 7am–2am, Sun
9am–1am

For a rustic farmhouse fix, snuggle up at this lounge-bar-restaurant hybrid. A comforting assortment of old armchairs and sofas, with wooden floorboards and timber-beamed ceilings, it's the kind of place you can happily while away a few lazy hours. Although you can breakfast, lunch or dine here, it's best for a coffee, tea or a pre-dinner libation. I especially love retreating to its cosy interior on dark, rainy afternoons, sitting by the crackling fireplace, sipping tea (alas, they use teabags, not loose-leaf), reading or working on my laptop (wi-fi is available). Didn't bring a book? You'll find a few stacked on the shelves. Other good times to drop by are on Monday and Thursday evenings, when live jazz or blues gets everyone's fingers and toes tapping.

9.

G-BAR

Piazza di Pasquino 69
06 6880 1085
Open Mon–Sun 8am–12am

Lovers of Italian design fawn over G-Bar, the street-fronting cafe-bar of boutique hotel G-Rough. You'll find lights by the great architect and industrial designer Gio Ponti, a credenza featuring the work of painter Piero Fornasetti in the back room, as well as specially commissioned wallpaper by Roman artist Pietro Ruffo. My favourite feature is the bathroom, a slightly surreal experience thanks to London-based Italian artist Davide D'Elia. The front room is lined with bronze-tinted Seletti glass tiles, setting a dramatic scene for a daytime caffè (coffee), best sipped in a 1960s Italian leather armchair while browsing a design magazine. From 6pm the venue switches to bar mode, when boutique Italian wines and seamlessly made martinis create a civilised spot for a pre-dinner swill. The hotel is one of the hottest spots to slumber in town, each of its 10 rooms graced with iconic Italian design and intriguing artworks. Fans include Australian fashion royal Collette Dinnigan, who featured it in *Vogue Australia*.

10.

CAFFETTERIA CHIOSTRO DEL BRAMANTE

Via Arco della Pace 5
06 6880 9036
www.chiostrodelbramante.it
Open Mon–Fri 10am–8pm,
Sat–Sun 10am–9pm

Not all museum cafes were created equal. Take the one hidden away on the first floor of the Chiostro del Bramante. Here, outdoor tables overlook a handsome Renaissance cloister designed by none other than Donato Bramante, one of Italy's greatest architects. Not that the cafe's assets stop there. The space includes a lofty corner lounge, speckled with comfy armchairs and sofas, and offering a view of Raphael's 1514 fresco *Sibyls*, which decorates the adjoining Chiesa di Santa Maria della Pace, also designed by Bramante. The lounge is popular with students and writers in search of a quiet space, and it's a soothing spot to escape the bustle of tourists below. I usually head here for a tranquil coffee and reading session, but the cafe also serves all-day bites, from cakes to panini, salads and warming dishes.

10.

10.

9.

Piazza Navona's architectural diva is the **Chiesa di Sant'Agnese in Agone**. Originally designed by Girolamo Rainaldi and his son, Carlo, the project was eventually entrusted to Baroque maestro Francesco Borromini. Its namesake St Agnes was reputedly martyred at the ancient **Stadio Domiziano**, which stood on this site, circa 304 CE. Ruins of the 1st-century stadium – the first masonry stadium built in the city – are accessible from Via di Tor Sanguigna, just north of Piazza Navona. The church itself hosts a number of music concerts each year; search www.classictic.com for upcoming events.

Fighting for attention outside the church is the monumental **Fontana dei Quattro Fiumi** (Fountain of the Four Rivers), created by Borromini's design arch rival Gian Lorenzo Bernini. Dating from 1651, the fountain's brawny protagonists represent the mighty Nile, Ganges, Danube and Plate rivers. At the southern end of the square, Bernini also contributed the statue of the Moor for the **Fontana del Moro** (Fountain of the Moor), created by Giacomo della Porta and completed in 1576. The fountain's four tritons are 19th-century copies.

The industrious Della Porta also created the basin for the **Fontana del Nettuno** (Neptune Fountain) at the northern end of Piazza Navona. The statues – which include mythical Roman god of the sea Neptune wrestling a sea monster – were added in the 19th century.

Hidden behind Piazza Navona's north-west corner is the curvaceous **Chiesa di Santa Maria della Pace** (Via Arco della Pace 5), home to Raphael's early 16th-century fresco *Sibille* (Sybyls). Flanking the church is Donato Bramante's chiostro (cloister), considered a masterpiece of High-Renaissance architecture. The cloister is now an evocative venue for temporary art exhibitions. Bramante reputedly lived a few blocks south, at Via del Governo Vecchio 123.

If you're craving more ancient beauty, don't miss the impressive **Museo Nazionale Romano: Palazzo Altemps** (Piazza Sant'Apollinare 44), a short walk north of Piazza Navona. The museum is home to an extraordinary collection of classical sculpture, including the 5th-century marble *Trono Ludovisi* (Ludovisi Throne) and the 2nd-century *Galata suicida* (Gaul's Suicide), the latter depicting an ill-fated, knife-clutching Gaul warrior grasping a dying woman. Basement drawcards include the foundations of a 4th-century BCE Roman domus (house) and the remnants of painted medieval walls. The museum also houses objects from the Museo Nazionale Romano's Egyptian collection.

PIAZZA DEL GESÙ

Piazza del Gesù

✠ CHIESA DEL GESÙ

VIA

DISPENSABILE

D'ARACOELI

TO MAP RIGHT
(ALONG VIA DELLE BOTTEGHE OSCURE &
PIAZZA DELL'ENCICLOPEDIA ITALIANA)

◀—

VIA   DELLE   BOTTEGHE   OSCURE

Roman and Jewish culture entwine in the Ghetto, one of the most beautiful (and least touristed) pockets of Rome's centro storico (historic centre). Established in 1555, this is the world's second oldest Jewish ghetto and home to Europe's second largest synagogue. Tranquil ochre-coloured side streets bend and slither either side of lively Via del Portico d'Ottavia, a cobbled, car-free strip filled with Jewish eateries, sun-seeking locals and gleeful Jewish-Roman school kids.

The neighbourhood's trattorias (casual restaurants) and bakeries are famous for their classic Jewish-Roman specialities, and a handful of idiosyncratic traders sell everything from luxury linens to rare organic chillies.

24   JUN 8076

SHOP
1 STAY
2 DISPENSABILE
3 PEPERITA
4 IL MUSEO DEL LOUVRE

EAT
5 PASTICCERIA BOCCIONE
6 BA'GHETTO

17

IL GHETTO
<u>AND</u> AROUND

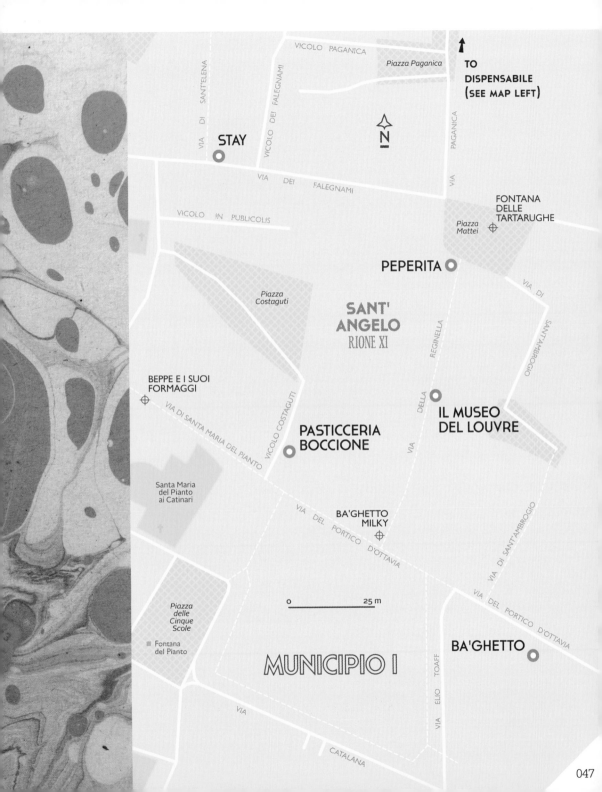

VICOLO PAGANICA

Piazza Paganica

TO
DISPENSABILE
(SEE MAP LEFT)

VIA DI SANT'ELENA

VICOLO DEI FALEGNAMI

VIA

STAY

N

VIA PAGANICA

VIA DEI FALEGNAMI

VICOLO IN PUBLICOLIS

FONTANA
DELLE
TARTARUGHE

*Piazza
Mattei*

PEPERITA

VIA DI

*Piazza
Costaguti*

**SANT'
ANGELO**
RIONE XI

VIA DELLA REGINELLA

VIA DI SANT'AMBROGIO

**BEPPE E I SUOI
FORMAGGI**

VIA DI SANTA MARIA DEL PIANTO

VICOLO COSTAGUTI

**PASTICCERIA
BOCCIONE**

**IL MUSEO
DEL LOUVRE**

Santa Maria
del Pianto
ai Catinari

VIA DEL PORTICO D'OTTAVIA

**BA'GHETTO
MILKY**

VIA DI SANT'AMBROGIO

0 ———— 25 m

VIA DEL PORTICO D'OTTAVIA

*Piazza
delle
Cinque
Scole*

■ Fontana
del Pianto

MUNICIPIO I

VIA ELIO TOAFF

BA'GHETTO

VIA

CATALANA

1.

STAY

Via dei Falegnami 63
334 2259695
http://staystore.it
Open Mon–Sat 10am–7pm

- -

Textile industry expert Ruben Fatucci and his partner, interior designer Alessandra Azzali, run this contemporary, pared-back linen store. Ruben – whose family owns the old textile store next door – sources high-quality natural fabrics from northern Italy to make their range of bedsheets, blankets, towels, tablecloths, runners, napkins and cushion covers. Fabrics are slow washed to soften both the material and the hues. Colours focus on restrained, muted shades like pale pink, terracotta, mustard, grey-blue and charcoal. I'm a big fan of the linen bedsheets, blended with cotton to make them softer and warmer on the skin. Best of all, each piece is sold separately, so you can mix and match for a distinctive, personalised look. I also love their presentation, simply and elegantly tied with string. Expect to pay between €140 and €200 for a duvet cover, depending on size – competitively priced for the quality, and made in Italy with the finest materials.

2

DISPENSABILE

Via d'Aracoeli 37–39
06 9826 1405
www.dispensabile.it
Open Mon–Sat 10.30am–1pm
& 1.30–7pm

- -

Architects Elena Cardilli, Sabrina Stante and Germana De Donno rule this temple to design, which doubles as their architecture studio. All distressed concrete walls and vintage tiles, its two levels showcase a sharp edit of furniture, homewares and other design objects. Brands run the gamut from Italian to international, meaning you're as likely to go gaga over an Ettore Sottsass–designed centrepiece as you are a geometric Danish serving tray, Finnish mugs or a French lamp. You'll find covetable objects for every room in your pad, from kitchen, lounge and study, to bedroom and bathroom. Upstairs is divided into a series of evocative rooms, which I like to pretend constitute my painfully cool Roman apartment. Despite the exclusiveness of the stock, you'll find items for varying budgets, making it a good spot to pick up something special for a style-savvy loved one (or just for yourself). You'll also find a small selection of cute women's threads from France's Des Petits Hauts.

3.

PEPERITA

Via della Reginella 30
392 4132158
http://peperita.it
Open Mon–Sun 10.30am–
1.45pm & 2.15–8pm

Like it hot? Get your kicks at
this fiery peperoncino (chilli)
peddler. You'll find 17 types
of chilli on sale here, offered
powdered, infused in olive
oil and unrefined sea salt, in
homestyle cooking sauces or
pâté, as well as jars of trito
fresco di peperoncino (chilli
puree), handy for adding
punch to your own finished
sughi (sauces). All the chillies
are biodynamic and grown at
owner Rita Salvatori's family
farm in Tuscany. Even the
olive oil is from the family
groves. Chillies are numbered
according to heat, from mild-
mannered Aji at number one
to hellfire Carolina Reaper
at 17. There's even a handy
chart indicating what types
of foods go best with each
chilli. My favourite product
here is the nifty pocket-sized
chilli wallet, lined with tiny
vials of various chillies you
can use to spice up your meal
anywhere, anytime. You'll
even find a chilli-infused
craft beer, made by Rita's
friends in Tuscany.

4.

IL MUSEO DEL LOUVRE

Via della Reginella 8A
06 6880 7725
www.ilmuseodellouvre.com
Open Mon–Sat 10.30am–7pm

It might be a fraction of the
size of that other Louvre, but
this little Ghetto time vault
bursts with cultural treasures.
More than a shop selling
photography, pre-loved books
and other vintage items,
it's a cultural archive. Its
collections of 30,000-plus
photographs include works
by some of Italy's most
celebrated 20th-century
photographers, among
them Ghitta Carrel, Luigi
Veronesi, Mario Schifano
and Tazio Secchiaroli.
Genres span everything from
reportage to film, fashion and
society, with no shortage of
intriguing, revealing shots
of anonymous figures and
cultural icons including
actors Sophia Loren and
Marcello Mastroianni, and
film director Pier Paolo
Pasolini. Old wooden
cabinets harbour other
time-warped snapshots,
including autographs and
the personal letters of 20th-
century intellectuals, poets
and writers. Chances are
you'll also stumble upon
vintage postcards, posters,
art tomes and back issues of
magazines such as *Domus*.
If you can pull yourself away,
climb the spiral staircase to
the first-floor gallery for the
photographic exhibitions.

3.

4.

4.

3.

3.

4.

5.

PASTICCERIA BOCCIONE

Via del Portico d'Ottavia 1
06 687 8637
Open Sun–Thurs 7am–7.30pm,
Fri 7am–3pm

The Ghetto's walls were still up when Boccione opened for business. Two centuries later, food lovers of all backgrounds squeeze into this tiny, spartan bakery for spectacular Jewish-Roman treats worth the infamously gruff service. The repertoire is limited but exceptional, from the amaretti (almond-paste biscuits) to the not-to-be-missed pizza ebraica – not actually a pizza, but a dense, charred slab of almond-paste biscuit jammed with almonds, pine nuts, raisins and chunks of candied fruit. If you're lucky, it'll still be warm from the oven. Even more spectacular is the crostata con ricotta e visciole, the Italian version of a tart, double crusted and bursting with light, fluffy ricotta and succulent sour cherries. As messy as it is to eat on the street, this is one of Rome's true culinary revelations, worth a stained top or ricotta-blotched shoe. Head in before lunch to ensure your share; Boccione's baked goods are highly prized and quick to vanish.

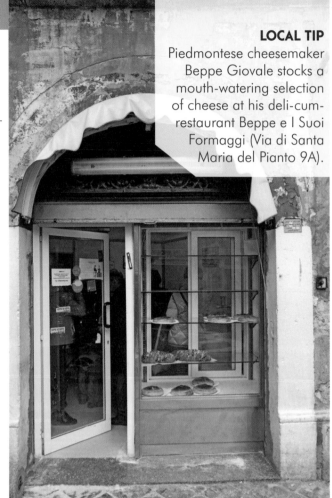

LOCAL TIP

Piedmontese cheesemaker Beppe Giovale stocks a mouth-watering selection of cheese at his deli-cum-restaurant Beppe e I Suoi Formaggi (Via di Santa Maria del Pianto 9A).

BA'GHETTO

Via del Portico d'Ottavia 57
06 6889 2868
www.baghetto.com
Open Sun–Thurs 12–11.30pm,
Fri 12–3pm, Sat 6–11.30pm

Opened by Jewish immigrants from Tripoli, this kosher kid is the best of the Jewish-Roman restaurants on Via del Portico d'Ottavia. The welcome is genuine, the decor smart, and the food fresh. My order always includes a serve of golden carciofi alla giudecca (Jewish-style artichokes), twice fried and irresistible. Other favourite prologues include tortino di aliciotti e indivia (anchovy and endive tart) and burik all'uovo, a delicate flaky pastry filled with runny egg yolk. Of the primi (first courses), Ba'Ghetto's couscous dishes stand out, while secondi (mains) range from baccalà (salted cod) and goulash to hardcore local offerings like coratella con carciofi (lamb's innards with artichokes). Epilogues include a choice of decent crostate (sweet pies), though if I'm lunching here I prefer to leave room for a slice of crostata con ricotta e visciole at nearby Pasticceria Boccione (*see* p. 052). Also down the street is Ba'Ghetto's sister restaurant Ba'Ghetto Milky, specialising in fish- and dairy-based dishes.

LOCAL TIP

Historic homewares store Leone Limentani (Via del Portico d'Ottavia 47) stocks coveted local and international porcelain, kitchenwares, designer lighting and more.

To learn about Jewish Rome's long, eventful, sometimes painful history, pay a visit to the **Museo Ebraico di Roma** (Jewish Museum; Via Catalana), located inside Rome's Great Synagogue. Exhibition topics include the Roman Razzia (Roman Round-up) of October 1943, which saw more than 2000 Roman Jews deported to concentration camps. Those who were taken and lost their lives are now commemorated with engraved bronze cobblestones scattered across the Ghetto, part of a pan-European memorial by Berlin artist Gunter Demnig.

The **Great Synagogue** is an eclectic mix of Greek and Assyrian influences crowned by Rome's only square-shaped dome. The museum also runs daily 45-minute tours of the neighbourhood; book tours at the ticket office.

East of the synagogue lie the ruins of the 11 BCE **Teatro di Marcello** (Via del Teatro di Marcello), a 20,000-seat arena fused into a 16th-century palazzo (large building) to striking effect. Standing beside it is the **Portico d'Ottavia**, a four-sided porch originally built by Augustus in 23 BCE and the site of the city's fish market from medieval times to the late 19th century.

Even older is the 62 BCE **Ponte Fabricio**, a pedestrian bridge connecting the Ghetto to the tiny **Isola Tiberina** (Tiber Island), one of the world's smallest inhabited islands and a good spot to get up close to what is Italy's third-longest river. Just off the southern tip of the island are the ruins of Rome's first stone bridge, the Pons Aemilius, brought to its knees by flood waters in 1598.

Back in the Ghetto, Piazza Mattei is worth a look for its adorable **Fontana delle Tartarughe** (Turtle Fountain), a late 16th-century work depicting four boys lifting turtles up into a basin. While the fountain is attributed to Giacomo della Porta and Taddeo Landini, the turtles were added by Gian Lorenzo Bernini in the mid-17th century.

Close by, the **Museo Nazionale Romano: Crypta Balbi** (Via delle Botteghe Oscure 31) is a veritable millefoglie of archaeological history, its multi-layered stratification revealing medieval buildings and, further below, the 13 BCE **Teatro di Balbo** (Balbo Theatre).

lla Porta designed the facade for the nearby **Chiesa del Gesù** (Piazza del Gesù), a Baroque tour de force whose electrifying ceiling frescoes – the work of Giovanni Battista Gaulli (Il Baciccia) – are worth a visit alone. The church's most famous resident is Spanish soldier, saint and Jesuits founder Ignatius Loyola, whose eternal resting place is a sumptuous tomb created by architect, artist and fellow Jesuit Andrea del Pozzo.

Trevi works it for the camera like few others. Immortalised in a string of classic films, its world-famous Fontana di Trevi (Trevi Fountain, see p. 066) draws torrents of swooning, coin-tossing admirers daily. From its base, medieval streets shoot out in a cinematic mix of shuttered windows and soft, earthy hues.

Among the touts and tacky souvenirs, locals go about their daily business: ministers consult on Quirinal Hill, corporate types negotiate at linen-clad tables, and teachers lead students through art-crammed palaces. From Piazza Barberini, leafy Via Vittorio Veneto snakes north towards Villa Borghese, recalling the 1950s and '60s when celebrities flocked here for Fellini-esque dolce vita.

24   JUN 80T6

SHOP
1 RINASCENTE

EAT
2 COLLINE EMILIANE
3 TEMAKINHO
4 IL GELATO DI SAN CRISPINO
5 MOMA

17

DRINK
6 IL GIARDINO RISTORANTE & BAR

TREVI, VIA VITTORIO VENETO <u>AND</u> AROUND

MUNICIPIO I

**CAMPO
MARZIO**
RIONE IV

VIALE DEL MURO TORTO

VIA DI PORTA PINCIANA

VIA LAZIO

VIA VITTORIO VENETO

VIA SARDEGNA

Grand Hotel
Via Veneto

Splendide
Royal

The
Westin
Excelsior

VIA LOMBARDIA

VIA EMILIA

Berg
Luxury

Hotel
Savoy

Baglioni
Hotel
Regina

0   100 m

**IL GIARDINO
RISTORANTE
& BAR**

LUDOVISI

Hotel
Caprice

SPAGNA

LUDOVISI
RIONE XVI

Hotel
Ambasciatori
Palace

CHIESA DELLA
TRINITÀ DEI MONTI

Sant'Isidoro
a Capole Case

VIA LIGURIA

N

Hotel
Majestic

VIA VITTORIO VENETO

MOMA

Piazza
Mignanelli

VIA SISTINA

VIA GREGORIANA

Hotel
Degli
Artisti

VIA DELLA PURIFICAZIONE

**CONVENTO DEI
CAPPUCCINI**

VIA DI SAN BASILIO

Hotel
Alexandra

Teatro
Salone
Margherita

Hotel
Elite

VIA SISTINA

Teatro
Sistina

VIA DI SAN NICOLA DA TOLENTINO

VIA BARBERINI

Basilica di
Sant'Andrea
delle Fratte

VIA DI CAPO LE CASE

Chic & Town
Luxury
Rooms

Galleria
d'Arte
Moderna

VIA ZUCCHELLI

BARBERINI

Sina
Bernini
Bristol

Teatro
Due Roma

Hotel La Fenice

Multisala
Barberini
(cinema)

**RINASCENTE &
TEMAKINHO**

**COLLINE
EMILIANE**

**PALAZZO
BARBERINI**

VIA DEL TRITONE

VIA DELLE QUATTRO FONTANE

TREVI
RIONE II

Hotel
de Petris

RASELLA

VIA DEL

**IL GELATO
DI SAN
CRISPINO**

VIA IN ARCIONE

VIA DEI GIARDINI

Giardini
del
Quirinale

**CHIESA DI SAN CARLO
ALLE QUATTRO FONTANE**

VIA DELLA PANETTERIA

QUIRINALE

Giardino di
Sant'Andrea
al Quirinale

**FONTANA
DI TREVI
(TREVI FOUNTAIN)**

Hotel
Fontana

Hotel
Trevi

Cortile
d'Onore

VIA DEL

Teatro dei
Dioscuri
al Quirinale

VIA DELLA DATARIA

**PALAZZO
DEL QUIRINALE**

1.

RINASCENTE

Via del Tritone 61
06 879 161
www.rinascente.it
Open Mon–Sun 9.30am–11pm

When Rinascente's flagship store opened in late 2017, Romans wryly muttered that they finally had a department store worthy of a capital city. They weren't wrong. The soaring atrium is a masterpiece, its grid-like form evoking both the city's Rationalist architecture and the restrained elegance of Giorgio Armani. Of course, it wouldn't be a Roman department store without ancient ruins in the basement – in this case, part of the Aqua Virgo aqueduct, launched by Augustus in 19 BCE. On the shopping front, expect both Italian and foreign luxe brands. The basement is good for cool Italian-design gifts, like a set of collectable Alessi teaspoons, while a few floors up, male style-council members will fawn over dress shirts from labels like Naples' Finamore. Brazilian–Japanese eatery Temakinho (*see* p. 060) is my pick of the eateries in the sixth-floor food hall. For a coffee or spritz (avoid the overpriced food), slip into Deco-inspired Up Sunset Bar, beyond which is a spectacular outdoor terrace with a view of Rome.

2.

COLLINE EMILIANE

Via degli Avignonesi 22
06 481 7538
www.collineemiliane.com
Open Tues–Sat 12.45–2.45pm & 7.30–10.45pm, Sun 12.45–2.45pm

Intimate, hospitable family-run Colline Emiliane flies the culinary flag for Emilia-Romagna, a northern Italian region famed for its culinary traditions. At linen-clad tables, politicians, business folk and clued-up gourmands tuck into fragrant cured meats, sharp formaggi (cheeses), and classic egg-based pasta primi (first courses) such as tagliatelle alla bolognese (long, flat ribbons of pasta served in a rich, meaty tomato ragù). Within 48 hours of landing in Rome, you will undoubtedly find me here, slurping gleefully on the superb tortellini in brodo (ring-shaped pasta filled with meat and served in a delicate broth). The silky egg-based pasta is made fresh daily in a glassed-off lab at the front of the restaurant. The secondi (mains) are a carnivorous affair, from milk-braised veal with velvety mashed potato to assorted boiled meats in salsa verde, while Sunday lunch is the time for the Latini family's revered bechamel-laced lasagne. Always book ahead.

1.

LOCAL TIP
From the sixth-floor food hall in Rinascente, outdoor stairs lead up to the rooftop for expansive views of Rome.

2.

3.

TEMAKINHO

Rinascente, Via del Tritone 61
06 8791 6660
www.temakinho.com
Open Mon–Sun 11.30am–11pm

The tropics have come to Rome at hotspot Temakinho, where jungle-themed wallpaper, sea-green ceramic tiles and Mid-Century accents set a lush, sophisticated scene for Brazilian–Japanese fusion fare. In the sixth-floor food hall of Rinascente's (*see* p. 058) flagship department store, you'll find super-fresh nosh, such as zingy ceviche de pescado (raw fish marinated in lime, red onion, peppers, chilli, garlic, coriander and ginger) and made-from-scratch sushi and temaki (hand rolls) filled with combos like salmon tartare with flying-fish caviar, avocado, fresh chives, sesame, sweet-and-sour sauce and spicy mayo. There's a good selection of vegetarian options, as well as fresh tropical smoothies, caipirinha cocktails (made with fresh fruit pulp) and Brazilian beers such as Brahma, Skol, Bohemia and Xingu to wash it all down. You'll find other branches in Monti and Borgo.

IL GELATO DI SAN CRISPINO

Via della Panetteria 42
06 679 3924
www.ilgelatodisancrispino.com
Open Sun–Thurs 11am–
12.30am, Fri–Sat 11am–
1.30am

Pity those tourists getting their licks in the gelaterie (ice-cream shops) just off Piazza di Trevi. A short walk away is the infinitely superior Gelato di San Crispino. Under these metal lids lies gelato so good that Pope John Paul II had it delivered to the Vatican. It is completely free of artificial powders and emulsifiers. In fact, everything here is made from scratch, using natural, premium ingredients such as unfiltered bitter honey from Sardinia, Amalfi lemons and Tahitian vanilla beans.

The flavour combinations themselves are inspired, from fresh walnut with dried fig, to zabaione with aged Marsala wine, to Calabrian liquorice. If you're a fan of liquorice, pair it with the mandarin for an icy revelation. Just don't go asking for a cone: the crew here are purists, arguing that cones detract from the flavour. It's a cup…or nothing.

5.

MOMA

Via di San Basilio 42
06 4201 1798
www.ristorantemoma.it
Open Mon–Sat 12.30–3pm &
7.30–11pm

Urbane Moma has two distinct personalities: a casual street-level bar and a finer-dining upstairs restaurant. Both are excellent. While the bar is the spot for espressos, artful pastries and eat-and-go tapas-style morsels, the linen-clad restaurant is for business lunches, lingering tete-a-tetes and swooning over refined takes on Italian classics. Try house-made gnocchi with cuttlefish ragù and marjoram, grilled wild octopus with variations on black salsify and tarragon, and a not-to-be-missed babà (rum-soaked sponge cake) with orange-and-pistachio cream. Moma takes food and hospitality seriously, from the quality of its produce to the attentiveness of its waitstaff (not always a given in this town). If the restaurant's neutral hues and restrained elegance have you thinking Armani, it's no coincidence: the space was inspired by the Milanese fashion deity, who also happens to be an old client. As for all those solid interior lines, they're a contemporary nod to the district's early 20th-century Rationalist architecture.

LOCAL TIP
For a satisfying on-the-go bite near Trevi Fountain, grab a panino (sandwich) at top-notch Pane e Salame (Via di Santa Maria in Via 19).

6.

IL GIARDINO RISTORANTE & BAR

Hotel Eden, Via Ludovisi 49
06 4781 2761
www.dorchestercollection.com/
en/rome/hotel-eden
Open Mon–Sun 7am–1am

It's not cheap, but life is short, you're in Rome, and the views are priceless. Perched on the sixth floor of the luxe Hotel Eden, this plush drinking den looks out over a tightly packed collection of rooftops, spires and domes, and the much-appreciated green of Villa Medici's gardens. While you could go for an espresso (€6), the cocktails (€23) last longer and are sensational. Take the negroni speziato (spiced negroni), with a dash of bergamot for added intrigue; or the out-of-the-box martini cacio e pepe, a classic vodka martini infused with pecorino romano cheese and black pepper, the flavours of Rome's classic pasta dish – it may sound disconcerting, but it's utterly gorgeous. Charming, perfectly preened staff are quick to replenish bowls of crisps, almonds and olives during aperitivo (6.30pm to 9pm). The restaurant is the domain of celebrated chef Fabio Ciervo; you may feel like a somewhat cheaper bite once your drinks bill arrives.

Dating from 1922, **Galleria Alberto Sordi** (Piazza Colonna) is one of the most beautiful shopping arcades in Italy. While your eyes will naturally gravitate towards the glorious stained-glass ceiling, take time to appreciate the detailed facade, adorned with ornamental garlands, pilasters, volutes and elegant Liberty-style lamps. The gallery's eponym is Rome's favourite home-grown actor, the late Alberto Sordi, who featured the gallery in his 1973 film classic *Polvere di stelle* (Stardust).

From Galleria Alberto Sordi, Via del Corso shoots south-east towards **Le Domus Romane di Palazzo Valentini** (Via Foro Traiano 85), subterranean ruins of Roman abodes brought back to life with a little help from multimedia displays. Book ahead (www.palazzovalentini.it) as guided tours alternate between Italian, English, French, Spanish and German.

A short walk east of Galleria Alberto Sordi is Baroque **Fontana di Trevi** (Trevi Fountain; Piazza di Trevi). Its protagonist is Greek god Oceanus, who rides a chariot pulled by a pair of seahorses, allegories for the sea's contrasting moods. Designed by Nicola Salvi and completed in 1762, the fountain is at its most alluring at night, when crowds have thinned and evening lights play on its travertine and water. Toss a coin into the fountain to secure your return to the Eternal City; just be sure to launch it over your left shoulder using your right hand. Note that eating and drinking on the steps leading down to the fountain is illegal and subject to an on-the-spot fine.

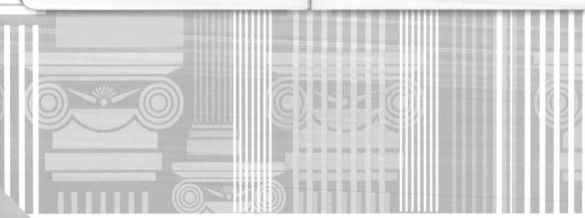

South of the fountain, Via della Dataria leads east to Piazza del Quirinale and colossal **Palazzo del Quirinale**, the world's ninth largest palace. Built in the 16th-century as a papal summer residence, it's now the pad of the Italian president. For a snoop inside, book a guided tour (in Italian only) at least five days ahead; tickets can be purchased online at http://palazzo.quirinale.it. Across the piazza lies the **Scuderie del Quirinale** (Via XXIV Maggio 16), former palace stables turned exhibition space.

From here, Via delle Quattro Fontane leads to 16th-century **Chiesa di San Carlo alle Quattro Fontane** (Via del Quirinale), the first church designed by Francesco Borromini. His genial use of convex and concave surfaces to create a sense of light and spaciousness in such a tiny space confirmed the architect's rare talent.

Borromini and Carlo Maderno are the hands behind nearby **Palazzo Barberini** (Via delle Quattro Fontane 13), a magnificent palazzo with a hefty booty of art that includes Caravaggio's *Giuditta e Oloferne* (Judith Beheading Holofernes) and *Narciso* (Narcissus). Don't forget to look up at Pietro da Cortona's show-stopping fresco *Il Trionfo della Divina Provvidenza* (Triumph of Divine Providence).

For something altogether more macabre, creep into nearby **Convento dei Cappuccini** (Via Vittorio Veneto 27), where human bones are put to creative use in bizarre crypt chapels.

In centuries past, glorious Piazza del Popolo (see p. 080) was the first impression most European travellers received of the Eternal City. Triangular neighbourhood Tridente shoots south off the square in a three-pronged formation of thoroughfares: Via Babuino draws fashion lovers and attitude with its arsenal of luxe boutiques; humbler Via di Ripetta serves up bakeries, wine bars, trattorias (casual restaurants) and other essentials; while Via del Corso lures texting teens with its global retail chains.

At the southern end of Tridente, A-list fashion heavyweights line salubrious Via Condotti, which spills into Piazza di Spagna, home to Rome's most famous alfresco staircase, the Spanish Steps (see p. 081).

24   JUN 8076

SHOP
1 MICHELEDILOCO
2 FONDACO
3 RE(F)USE
4 MONOCLE
5 ARTISANAL CORNUCOPIA
6 ENOTECA BUCCONE

EAT AND DRINK
7 ASSAGGIA
8 LA BUVETTE
DRINK
9 STRAVINSKIJ BAR

TRIDENTE AND PIAZZA DEL POPOLO

PIAZZA DEL POPOLO

CHIESA DI SANTA MARIA IN MONTESANTO

ARTISANAL CORNUCOPIA

Hotel Locarno

CHIESA DI SANTA MARIA DEI MIRACOLI

STRAVINSKIJ BAR

VIA ANGELO BRUNETTI

ENOTECA BUCCONE

Ripetta 25

CASA DI GOETHE

ASSAGGIA

Pincio

VIALE GABRIELE D'ANNUNZIO

VIALE DEL MURO TORTO

Villa Borghese

Villa Medici gardens

VIALE DELLA TRINITÀ DEI MONTI

Villa Medici

VIA DEL VANTAGGIO

VIA DEL BABUINO

Hotel Centrale

VIA DI SAN GIACOMO

VIA DEL CORSO

VIA DEI GRECI

VIA ANTONIO CANOVA

FONDACO

LA BUVETTE

PIAZZA AUGUSTO IMPERATORE

Mausoleo di Augusto

PIAZZA AUGUSTO IMPERATORE

CAMPO MARZIO

RIONE IV

VIA VITTORIA

VIA DELLA CROCE

PASTIFICIO GUERRA

Hotel Condotti

VIA BELSIANA

Piazza di Spagna

MARGUTTA

Hotel Art by the Spanish Steps

N

0   100 m

MUSEO DELL'ARA PACIS

Basilica dei Santi Ambrogio e Carlo al Corso

Grand Hotel Plaza

VIA DELLA BOCCA DI LEONE

VIA DELLE CARROZZE

ANTICO CAFFÉ GRECO

KEATS-SHELLEY HOUSE

Spanish Steps

VIA DEI CONDOTTI

VIA

VIA TOMACELLI

Fontana del Porto di Ripetta

VIA DELL'ARANCIO

VIA DEL CORSO

ZUMA

BORGOGNONA

RE(F)USE

Piazza Borghese

VIA DELLA FONTANELLA DI BORGHESE

MICHELEDILOCO

FRATTINA

Hotel Homs

VIA MARIO DE' FIORI

VIA DI RIPETTA

CAMPO MARZIO

Basilica di San Lorenzo in Lucina

VIA DELLA VITE

VIA DELLA MERCEDE

MUNICIPIO I

Nuovo Olimpia (cinema)

Teatro Sala Umberto

VIA DEL CORSO

Hotel Adriano

MONOCLE

Piazza del Parlamento

Piazza di San Silvestro

VIA DEL TRITONE

1.

MICHELEDILOCO

Via del Leone 7
06 4547 9103
www.micheledioco.it
Open Mon 3.30–7.30pm,
Tues–Sat 10.30am–7.30pm,
Sun 11am–7.30pm

Carrie Bradshaw would
hyperventilate at
Michelediloco. Less a shoe
store and more a gallery of
shoe-making at its finest,
this is a place for all things
artisanal: striking, hard-
to-find and avant-garde
footwear displayed on timber
shelves that seemingly
pop out of the wall. Satisfy
your hankering for a pair of
black boots with lipstick-red
'plastic cup' heels, trekking
boots with a sexy urban
twist or cardinal-red dress
shoes in dramatic cracked
leather. A passion for kicks
drives owners Michele and
Manuela, whose affability
extends to a bar fridge
stocked with beer. Coveted
brands include Italy's Officine
Creative, Moma and Marsell.
Bags designed by the latter
are also on offer, alongside
contemporary men's and
women's jewellery from
designers such as Florence-
based Manuel Bozzi. Another
plus is the selection of niche
fragrances from meisters
Mirko Buffini and Paris-based
Australian Naomi Goodsir.
Shoes retail from around
€300 for women and €330 for
men, with sneakers starting
circa €190.

2.

FONDACO

Via della Frezza 43
06 9209 8856
http://fondacoroma.com
Open Mon–Sun 11am–7.30pm

Fondaco has turned the
high-end concept store
into a concept street, its
numerous departments
sporting separate shopfronts
on Via della Frezza. You'll
find a green-hued tearoom
(complete with rotating
photography exhibitions),
with an adjacent restaurant,
contemporary gallery, art
library, basement spa and a
trio of eclectic luxury suites.
The **Home Design** store
stocks Danish and Japanese
stationery, exclusive French
and Italian kitchenware
and leather duffels, while
the record-peddling **Vinyl
Room** is curated by singer-
songwriter Francesco
De Gregori. Pop into the
Outdoor store for Danish
knitwear, men's portable
grooming kits, handmade
bikes from Brooks, and a
range of backpacks and
sunglasses designed by
Luca Morganti; the specs are
made using wood from old
Venetian bricole (navigation
marker poles). The **Home
Collection** store stocks
heavenly Castellini linens,
while the **Boutique** focuses
on high-end female fashion
from designers like Capucci
and Rochas. There's even a
dedicated **Pet Shop**, with
Nordic labels and a toilette
for pooches.

1.

2.

2.

1.

1.

2.

3.

RE(F)USE

Via della Fontanella di
Borghese 40
06 6813 6975
www.carminacampus.com/refuse
Open Mon 3–7.30pm, Tues–Sat
10am–7.30pm

LOCAL TIP
Style up for rooftop bar
Zuma (Palazzo Fendi,
Via della Fontanella di
Borghese 48) earlier in
the week to avoid the
weekend masses.

Recycling reaches exhilarating heights at Re(f)use, the passion project of designer Ilaria Venturini Fendi. Her label Carmina Campus transforms everything from old life vests, shirts, cycling jerseys, fabric swatches and even Coke cans into covetable, high-end handbags, totes and more. Ilaria's Fendi pedigree is evident in the impeccable artisanship, with each piece made in Italy using highly specialised skills. Collaborative projects include a Made in Prison line, which sees people serving time in Italian prisons taught the necessary skills to manufacture the bags and partly support themselves. Re(f)use also showcases other talented designers focused on recycling and sustainability. The accessories on offer are equally fantastical, whether it's old keys turned into necklaces, leather swatches transformed into wallets, or soft-drink tabs reimagined as modern takes on Victorian rings. Bags start from around €150. Don't forget to look up to appreciate British designer Stuart Haygarth's centrepiece chandelier, made using old spectacles.

MONOCLE

4.

MONOCLE
Via di Campo Marzio 13
06 683 3668
www.monocle.it
Open Mon–Sat 10.30am–
7.30pm, Sun 11.30am–7.30pm

Yearning to sell eyewear he actually liked, third-generation optician Gabriele Vergerio branched out to open his own custom-design eyewear store. Needless to say, the guy has fine taste, stocking some of the world's most coveted independent luxury brands, among them Ahlem from France, Matsuda from Japan and Italy's Kuboraum. Monocle's own exclusive eyewear line includes 14 models of sunglasses, all handmade in the Veneto region. Sunglasses retail from around €150, with Monocle's own creations ranging from €270 to €330. Prescription lenses take one day for single-vision, or four to five days for progressive and bifocal. A small, curated range of accessories includes sleek Claustrum cardholders from Tokyo and spectacular fragrances from Italian perfumer Meo Fusciuni. Like what you smell? It's Monocle's own ambient scent, created in collaboration with high-end perfumery Campomarzio70. And, yes, you can purchase that too.

5.

ARTISANAL CORNUCOPIA

Via dell'Oca 38
342 8714597
www.artisanalcornucopia.com
Open Mon 3.30–7.30pm,
Tues–Sat 10.30am–7.30pm,
Sun 4.30–7.30pm

This little gem of a shop celebrates high-end artisanal objects from Rome, Italy and beyond. Charismatic owner Elif Emine Sallorenzo – who substituted life as a New York attorney for a more creative existence in Rome – describes the space as 'positive globalisation', and stocks some of the world's unique and most intriguing creative talent. To date, Cornucopia has showcased handmade jewellery by Giulia Barela (exhibited at New York's Museum of Art and Design), pop-abstract handbags by Seattle-born, Bologna-based Tonya Hawkes, and seamless sculptural sunglasses from Turin's Ninali. It was the first store in Italy to stock Cangiari, a completely organic, anti-Mafia fashion line from Calabria that uses ancient textile-making techniques from Magna Grecia and Byzantine. It was also the first to stock the relaunched line of classic unisex fragrances by French fashion deity Jacques Fath. Elif stocks her own limited-edition line of mechanic-style jumpsuits, too (yes, guys, you can wear them).

6.

ENOTECA BUCCONE

Via di Ripetta 19–20
06 361 2154
www.enotecabuccone.com
Open Mon–Fri 10am–9.30pm,
Sat 10am–11pm, Sun
11am–7pm

One of the few spots near Piazza del Popolo that doesn't feel like a tourist circus, this dark, woody wine shop and bar is a time-warped whirl of vintage mirrors and yesteryear props, from an old barrel-carrying wooden cart to a giant, handmade wooden fridge (the latter still in use). Carved floor-to-ceiling wine shelves gleam with well-chosen, predominately Italian wines. Sibling owners Vincenzo and Francesco Buccone offer drops from a few smaller winemakers, too, including Forchir and Luisa from Italy's north-eastern Friuli region. For something super-local, seek out a bottle from Gelso della Valchetta, a winery located within Rome's city limits. The wine bar has a scattering of tables for the lunch crowd, which noshes on Roman comfort staples such as fantastic pasta e fagioli (pasta with beans) and lighter summertime fare including insalata di mare (seafood salad). From 5pm, Buccone goes into aperitivo mode, offering wine degustations with accompanying nibbles.

5.

6.

7.

ASSAGGIA

Margutta 19, Via Margutta 19
06 9779 7980
www.assaggiaroma.com
Open Mon–Sun 12.30–2.30pm
& 7.30–11pm

Headed by Michelin-starred chef Angelo Troiani, plush Assaggia is nestled inside Margutta 19, a boutique hotel on scandalously handsome Via Margutta. The restaurant's name translates as 'taste', which is precisely what its tapas-like menu offers: smaller 'tastings' of tweaked Roman classics such as supplì al telefono (mozzarella-and-minced-meat-stuffed risotto balls), slow-cooked pollo e peperoni (chicken with diced peppers) and frittata con zucchini, fiori di zucca e mentuccia (zucchini, zucchini flower and Roman mint frittata). Bites also include salumi (cured meats), cheeses and carpaccio (raw fish) dishes, all of which are offered in set tasting menus that range from four to nine dishes, with extra 'tastes' available. Even the desserts follow the format, with a trio of tastings that might include dangerously addictive bombe fritte (fried doughnuts filled with vanilla cream). Lush lounges and an outdoor terrace make Assaggia the perfect place for a civilised cocktail session among Rome's moneyed bella gente (beautiful people).

LOCAL TIP
Time-warped pasta shop Pastificio Guerra (Via della Croce 8) serves lunchtime pasta with wine daily for €4 (cash and standing-room only).

8.

LA BUVETTE

Via Vittoria 44
06 679 0383
Open Mon–Sat 8am–11pm, Sun
9am–11pm

As the name suggests, there's a deliciously French vibe at La Buvette, an all-day bistro-bar with handsome barkeeps, tables on a cobbled-street and an expansive menu that dabbles in numerous cuisines. Arrive for morning pancakes, eggs Benedict or buttery house croissants, or head in later in the day for a burger or salad combos that might see boiled shrimp tossed in with artichokes, pear and Parmigiano-Reggiano. While meals are generally good, I mostly go for the aperitivo (5pm to 8pm), when well-mixed drinks are served with quality nibbles, from addictive potato crisps made in-house to moreish tartines topped with eggplant, cured meat and cream cheese. Head barkeep Alessandro Spennato takes his mixology seriously, a fact reflected in La Buvette's intriguing, often brilliant repertoire of cocktails. My pick: The Gentleman, a sultry, smoky cross between an old fashioned and a negroni, served in a glass skull that makes the smoke look rather cerebral. No reservations; go early or patiently toe-tap.

9

LOCAL TIP

Sip standing at the bar to save euros at Antico Caffé Greco (Via Condotti 86), Rome's oldest cafe, its former regulars including Casanova and Goethe.

STRAVINSKIJ BAR

Hotel de Russie, Via del Babuino 9
06 3288 8874
www.roccofortehotels.com/hotels-and-resorts/hotel-de-russie
Open Mon–Sun 9am–1am

You don't need keys to a suite to indulge at Rome's luxe Hotel de Russie. Its plush Stravinskij Bar is a decadent spot for a cappuccino or, better still, a flawless cocktail. Sit in the swoon-inducing courtyard, where sun-shaded tables and a backdrop of terraced gardens practically beg for Gucci shades and a little Roman attitude. Your martini may see gin filtered over jasmine green tea and lifted with a drop of St Germain elderflower liqueur. The choice of gin and tonics is equally inspired: should you opt for the cucumber and Bulgarian roses, or ditch the gin altogether for a Mediterranean twist pairing organic vodka and tonic with sun-dried cherry tomatoes and basil? I especially love perching here for pre-dinner aperitivo: the bar snacks are suitably posh and the scene an entertaining mix of air kisses, surgical enhancements and high fashion: is that Gucci, Prada or Fendi? Expect to pay around €22 for a martini, but the quality is high and the setting fabulous.

Piazza del Popolo is one of Rome's most spectacular squares, its current design the work of Neoclassical architect Giuseppe Valadier. The piazza's southern end is framed by Carlo Rinaldi's almost-identical 17th-century churches, **Chiesa di Santa Maria dei Miracoli** and **Chiesa di Santa Maria in Montesanto**. Its most fascinating church, however, is early Renaissance **Basilica di Santa Maria del Popolo** (Piazza del Popolo 12), located on the piazza's northern side. Treasures here include two Caravaggio masterpieces – the *Conversion of St Paul* and the *Crucifixion of St Peter* – as well as frescoes by Pinturicchio.

While the current **Porta del Popolo** – the city gate beside the basilica – dates back to Jubilee Year 1475, its southern facade was added by Bernini in 1655 to celebrate Queen Christina of Sweden's controversial conversion to Catholicism. Piercing the square's belly is an ancient Egyptian **obelisk**, brought to Rome by Augustus and originally shown off at chariot racecourse Circo Massimo.

From Piazza del Popolo, Via di Ripetta leads to **Museo dell'Ara Pacis** (Lungotevere in Auga). Its prized possession is the 13 BCE Ara Pacis Augustae (Altar of Peace). An epic marble altar carved with pseudo-historical and allegorical reliefs, it's considered one of the most important works of Ancient Roman sculpture in existence. The altar's contemporary glass and travertine pavilion – designed by American architect Richard Meier and completed in 2003 – was the first modern civic building erected in Rome's historic centre since World War II. Its addition stirred no shortage of controversy, with detractors comparing it to everything from a coffin to a petrol station.

Those who enjoy snooping around the former abodes of literary greats have two options in Tridente. **Casa di Goethe** (Via del Corso 18) accommodated Johann Wolfgang von Goethe from 1786 to 1788, and its collection of memorabilia includes letters and sketches by the great German writer. More letters and personal artefacts await at **Keats-Shelley House** (Piazza di Spagna 26), where English poet John Keats and painter Joseph Severn lived from late 1820 until Keats' untimely death in early 1821.

Piazza di Spagna is home to world-famous 18th-century staircase the **Spanish Steps**, designed by the late-Baroque architect Francesco de Sanctis. Its sweep of 135 steps leads up to the 16th-century **Chiesa della Trinità dei Monti** (Piazza Trinità dei Monti 3), commissioned by Louis XII of France and home to beautiful frescoes by Mannerist artist Daniele da Volterra. If the crowds get too much, head north on Via Babuino for one block, turn right into Via Albert and take a quiet wander along beautiful **Via Margutta**, an elegant strip once home to Italian film-directing great Federico Fellini (who lived at number 110).

PONTE RISORGIMENTO

MUSEO ETRUSCO VILLA GIULIA

BELLE ARTI

VIA DI VILLA GIULIA

VILLA PONIATOWSKI

MUSEO NAZIONALE ETRUSCO

Fiume Tevere

VIA DELLE NAVI

VIA GAETANO FILANGIERI

LUNGOTEVERE DELLE NAVI

VIA FLAMINIA

PINCIANO QUARTIERE III

MINISTERO MARINA

Mercatino del Borghetto Flaminio

L'ANTICA PIZZERIA DA MICHELE

VIA FLAMINIA

AZUNI/ MIN.MARINA

VIA GIUSEPPE

VIA DEGLI SCIALOJA

VIA DEGLI PISANELLI

FLAMINIO

ARANCIA BLU

PONTE PIETRO NENNI

VIA CESARE BECCARIA

FLAMINIO

FLAMINIO

Bordered by 15th-century city gate Porta del Popolo to the south, the River Tiber to the north and west, and the Monti Parioli to the east, leafy, low-key Flaminio lacks the cobbled, centuries-old charm of Rome's historic core. Instead it's home to modern landmarks, from contemporary cultural hubs designed by A-list architects to Mid-Century Olympic architecture.

Its main north–south thoroughfare is Via Flaminia, an ancient military road that once led the Romans north towards the Apennines and the Adriatic Sea. Let it lead you to contemporary art collections, concert halls and a small but worthy handful of thoughtful, neighbourly cafes, wine bars and eateries.

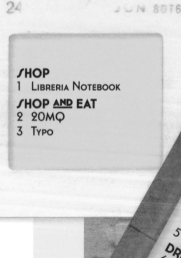

24   JUN 8076

SHOP
1 LIBRERIA NOTEBOOK

SHOP AND EAT
2 20MQ
3 TYPO

17

EAT
4 Lo'STERIA
5 PASTICCERIA MONDI

DRINK
6 MOSTÓ

FLAMINIO AND AROUND

TORDI QUINTO
QUARTIERE XVIII

Chiesa della
Gran Madre
di Dio

⊙ **PASTICCERIA
MONDI**

LO'STERIA
⊙

VIA CASSIA

CORSO DI FRANCIA

VIALE DI TORDI QUINTO

N

0   200 m

PONTE FLAMINIO

(River   Tiber)

VIA DEI ROBILANT

LUNGOTEVERE MARESCIALLO DIAZ

**PONTE
MILVIO**   Fiume   Tevere

⊕

LUNGOTEVERE
SALVO D'ACQUISTO

LUNGOTEVERE
DELL'ACQUA ACETOSA

LUNGOTEVERE GRANDE
AMMIRAGLIO THAON DI REVEL

VIA DEGLI OLIMPIONICI

VIA DEGLI OLIMPIONICI

VIA STATI UNITI D'AMERICA

VIA PORTOGALLO

CORSO DI FRANCIA

VIA GERMANIA

**CROCETTE-
VIA TURCHIA**

PINTURICCHIO

MOSTÓ ⊙ 🚊

🚊 **TIZIANO/
XVII OLIMPIADE**

PARIOLI
QUARTIERE II

Piazza
Antonio
Mancini

MANCINI
🚊 🚊

VIALE PINTURICCHIO

VIA FLAMINIA

VIA GUGLIELMO CALDERINI

VIALE XVII   OLIMPIADE

VIALE XVII   OLIMPIADE

VIA CANADA

**CROCETTE-
VIA DANEMARCA**

Villa
Glori

CARRACCI
🚊

VIA MASACCIO

✉

VIA TIZIANO

🚹🚺

**LIBRERIA
NOTEBOOK**
⊙

⊕

**AUDITORIUM
PARCO DELLA
MUSICA**

**FLAMINIA/
RENI**
🚊

**PALAZZETTO
DELLO
SPORT**

⊕

⊕

**MAXXI:
MUSEO NAZIONALE
DELLE ARTI
DEL XXI SECOLO** ⊕⊙ **TYPO**

🚊 **APOLLODORO**

■ Museo
Archeologico

RENI

VIA GUIDO

VIA RENI

VIALE TIZIANO

Stadio
Flaminio

MARESCIALLO PILSUDSKI

FLAMINIO
QUARTIERE I

MUNICIPIO II

VIALE DEL VIGNOLA

VIA FLAMINIA

Villa
Elia

20MQ ⊙

**FLAMINIA/
FRACASSINI**
🚊

🚊 **ANKARA/TIZIANO**

VIALE TIZIANO

VIALE

LUNGOTEVERE FLAMINIO

FLAMINIO

■ Best Western
Hotel Astrid

1.

LIBRERIA NOTEBOOK

Viale Pietro de Coubertin 30
06 8069 3461
Open Mon–Sun 10am–8.30pm

Rome's iconic Auditorium Parco della Musica (*see* p. 092) sets an appropriate scene for this sprawling book and music store. While most titles are in Italian, you will find a good selection of English-language books about Rome and its history, as well as notable booty focused on art, photography and architecture. The appetite-piquing selection of culinary tomes also includes a handful of English-language options, including food-critic guides to the city's eateries. Those who read Italian will find a fantastic selection of books about Italian wines, not to mention a bounty of both classic and contemporary fiction and non-fiction titles. One section is entirely dedicated to gialli (detective novels). Music lovers will find a weighty selection of Italian- and English-language CDs, plus sheet music and a robust selection of DVDs spanning Stanley Kubrick box sets to classic and contemporary Italian cinema.

LOCAL TIP
If you prefer doughier Neapolitan pizza to Rome's crispier, thinner version, tuck in at L'Antica Pizzeria Da Michele (Via Flaminia 82).

2

20MQ

Via Flaminia 314C
06 3105 2302
http://20mq.com
Open Mon–Sun 8am–10pm

Fancy those filament bulbs? The wallpaper? Perhaps the chair you're sitting on? Almost everything in sight is for sale at this laid-back cafe and design store. It's the brain child of Massimiliano Rubcich and Emanuele Vitale, the former a trained architect. Timber shelves are stacked with an eclectic collection of designer gifts – wallets, bags and novelty items – from Lithuania, Israel, Japan and beyond. Emerging local designers are also commonly showcased. 20MQ is a fantastic spot to sip single-origin coffee, freshly squeezed juices and natural vino, or to fill up from a healthy, worldly, organic menu. It's where I head for a serious hit of vitamins in the form of a poke bowl with vegetables, a spelt soup with wilted greens or an avocado salad. Massimiliano stops by the market at Ponte Milvio each morning, picking out quality produce for his cooks to use. Stacks of magazines, free wi-fi and friendly staff encourage carefree lingering.

LOCAL TIP
Flaminio is home to one of the city's best-loved vegetarian restaurants, Arancia Blu (Via Cesare Beccaria 3).

3.

TYPO

MAXXI, Via Guido Reni 4A
06 9432 0661
www.maxxi.art
Open Tues–Fri & Sun
8am–9pm, Sat 8am–10pm

- -

There are many reasons to love white-on-white cafe and design store Typo. Firstly, it sits inside the Zaha Hadid–designed art museum MAXXI (*see* p. 092), whose Kubrick-esque interior is unmissable. Secondly, it's spacious, with an ample mix of tables, communal bar tables and armchairs encouraging you to linger (the wi-fi is reliable and free). Thirdly, the affable staff serves up some of the best coffee in this part of town. You'll also find freshly squeezed juices, wine, beer and cocktails, not to mention pastries, muffins, fruit salads and panini (the latter a hit-and-miss affair). Together, these things draw everyone from international museum visitors to keyboard-tapping creatives and students. In between drinks, browse the giftshop shelves. Books range from art, design and film to Rome itself, and an eclectic mix of design gifts and knick-knacks can include graphic-print mugs, notebooks and stationery, ceramics and lighting, retro-inspired sunglasses, photographic prints of the city, and even kooky iron-on patches.

4.

LO'STERIA

Via dei Prati della Farnesina 61
06 3321 8749
www.lo-steria.it
Open Tues–Sun 12.30–2.30pm
& 7.30–11.30pm

Brothers Andrea and Luca Ogliotti run this modern osteria (casual restaurant), a short walk across the River Tiber from Flaminio. It's an honest, bustling place, with butcher-paper placemats, tin lamps and friendly waitstaff. While Andrea manages front of house, Luca cooks up simple, flavour-packed Roman home-cooking. The golden frittura (tempura-style vegetables) make for a satisfying antipasto while the comforting primi (first courses) include a decent tonnarelli cacio e pepe (pasta with pecorino romano and coarse black pepper). Secondi (mains) are equally nostalgic, whether it's succulent salsiccia e broccoletti (pork sausage with broccolini) or polpette in sugo (meatballs in tomato sauce). If it's on the menu, the salsiccia di cioccolato (chocolate 'sausage') makes for a deliciously cheeky final act. Before leaving, check out the fascinating vintage photographs of Rome. Book ahead for dinner or Sunday lunch.

5.

PASTICCERIA MONDI

Via Flaminia Vecchia 468
06 333 6466
Open Tues–Sun 7am–9.30pm

This classic Roman pastry shop is etched into the childhood memories of many a Roman friend of mine. One of these friends got me hooked on Mondi's gelato, which I love as much for the names of the flavours as for the taste. Cult favourites here include the Eroe due mondi (Hero Two Worlds), a combo of white chocolate, meringue and granella (grains), and the aptly titled Indispensabile (Essential), a blend of zabaglione, croccante (brittle) and crumbed pistachio. Then there's the Insuperabile (Invincible), a refreshing mix of lemon cream, wild strawberries, meringue and crumbed pistachio. Fridges lure with their trays of adorable mondini, mini-sized gelato lollipops in flavours such as Nutella, marron glacé (glazed candied chestnut) and cocco (coconut). Iced confections aside, you'll find a long counter laden with breakfast cornetti, colourful pastries and savoury lunchtime bites such as brioche-like mini panini. Somewhat less appealing is the drab outdoor seating area, a likely candidate for a TV home-reno show.

4.

5.

6.

MOSTÓ
Viale Pinturicchio 32
392 2579616
Open Tues–Sat 6.30pm–2am,
Sun 6pm–2am (Mon–Sat
Jun–Aug)

Mostó is the kind of wine
bar everyone wants at the
end of their street. Low-key
and personable, it focuses its
energy on genuine human
interaction and the pouring
of intriguing, mostly natural
wines. Regulars sit at the
timber bar, catching up on
neighbourhood gossip and
bantering with Neapolitan
co-owner Ciro Borriello.
There's no wine list here; Ciro
will simply plonk a number
of options on your table,
based on personal tastes and
budget. Wines by the bottle
start from around €20, and
span the globe, from Italy and
France, to Austria, Germany,
the Czech Republic, South
Africa and Argentina. Nibbles
are unfussy, ranging from
platters of formaggi (cheeses)
and salumi (cured meats), to
tapas-sized bread slices with
toppings such as ciauscolo, a
spreadable salami hailing from
the Le Marche region. For a
sweet-and-sour fix, order the
classic Neapolitan insalata
di rinforzo, a salad of pickled
vegetables and anchovies that
I find difficult to resist. The
kitchen closes at 12am.

Rising a short walk east of Via Flaminio is architect Renzo Piano's **Auditorium Parco della Musica** (Viale Pietro de Coubertin 30), a rare example of contemporary architecture in the city. If you find yourself comparing its trio of pod-like concert halls to armadillos or computer mice, you won't be the first. For deeper insight into the place, take one of the one-hour weekend guided tours (in Italian unless English requested in advance). Alternatively, take a low-key snoop yourself. The complex houses several small, free museums and exhibition spaces, including one that showcases artefacts from an Ancient Roman farm and villa uncovered on the site, and another that displays historical musical instruments. See the website (https://en.auditorium.com) for tours and museum opening hours.

The website also lists upcoming concerts, which run the gamut from classical to jazz and rock, from both homegrown and international artists.

A quick walk west of Via Flaminio leads to the Zaha Hadid-designed **MAXXI: Museo Nazionale delle Arti del XXI Secolo** (Via Guido Reni 4A). Hosting contemporary art exhibitions throughout the year, the museum took over a decade to construct. Inaugurated in 2010, the wait was worth it: its space-age interiors – complete with suspended stairs and walkways – are simply breathtaking.

Directly north of Auditorium Parco della Musica lie relics of the 1960 Summer Olympics. These include the UFO-like **Palazzetto dello Sport** (Piazza Apollodoro 10), its unusual thin-shell concrete dome the work of renowned Italian

engineer and architect Pier Luigi Nervi. It also includes housing from one of the world's first purpose-built Olympic villages. The best of the lot is the so-called **Crocette**, the elevated, crisscross-plan buildings on Via Danemarca and Via Turchia.

Crossing the River Tiber at Flaminio's northern edge is **Ponte Milvio**, a bridge that marks the very spot where Christian-convert Constantine the Great defeated Maxentius in 312 CE. The victory played a major role in leading Europe towards Christianity.

Across the river from Flaminio is the **Foro Italico** (Viale del Foro Italico), a sports complex inspired by the forums of ancient Rome's Imperial Age. Built between 1928 and 1938, the complex was originally known as the Foro Mussolini, in honour of Italy's Fascist leader Benito Mussolini. While the name has changed, the Foro remains one of the Rome's most important examples of Italian Fascist architecture. Its buildings include the **Stadio Olimpico** (Olympic Stadium), the main site of the 1960 Summer Olympics and a popular venue for big-name touring music acts (yes, even Beyoncé has roused the crowds here).

Set snugly in a left-bank curve of the River Tiber, bohemian Trastevere is the stuff of Instagram dreams: cobbled, largely car-free streets; ivy-tickled buildings; and heart-stealing piazzas (squares) speckled with fountains, medieval churches and free-spirited cafes. Despite its proximity to the city centre, Trastevere has always been a place apart. An enclave for Jews, Syriacs, sailors and slaves during the Roman Republic, it wasn't until the 14th century that Rome finally embraced it as an official rione (city district).

Centuries on, Trastevere remains deeply cosmopolitan, its vintage trattorias (casual eateries), late-night bars and eclectic boutiques drawing artists, students and hedonists from all over.

24   JUN 8016

SHOP
1 Antica Caciara Trasteverina
2 Verso Sud
3 Marta Ray
4 Elvis Lives
5 OFF–Roma

17

EAT
6 Le Levain
7 Da Enzo
8 Fernanda

EAT AND DRINK
9 Alembic

DRINK
10 Enoteca Ferrara

TRASTEVERE AND AROUND

BEPPE E I SUOI FORMAGGI

BA'GHETTO MILKY

ARENULA/ MIN. G. GIUSTIZIA

MUSEO EBRAICO DI ROMA (JEWISH MUSEUM OF ROME)

LUNGOTEVERE DELLA FARNESINA

LUNGOTEVERE DEI VALLATI

ARENULA

PONTE SISTO

Fontana di Ponte Sisto

BIR & FUD

Fiume Tevere

Isola Tiberina (Tiber Island)

PONTE FABRICIO

ENOTECA FERRARA

LUNGOTEVERE RAFFAELLO SANZIO

PONTE GARIBALDI

ISOLA TIBERINA

Piazza Fatebenefratelli

VIA DELLA SCALA

MARTA RAY

VIA DELLA PELLICCIA

TRASTEVERE

RIONE XIII

BELLI

LUNGOTEVERE DEGLI ANGUILLARA

Piazza di Sant'Egidio

BASILICA DI SANTA MARIA IN TRASTEVERE

San Crisogono

Reale (cinema)

ALEMBIC

Piazza in Piscinula

Piazza di San Calisto

BAR SAN CALISTO

VIA DELLA LUCE

BISCOTTIFICIO INNOCENTI

VIA DEI

VIA

LUCIANO MANARA

VIA DI SAN FRANCESCO

VIA DEI FIENAROLI

VIA DI SAN GALLICANO

TRASTEVERE

DA ENZO

GENOVESI

ANTICA CACIARA TRASTEVERINA

BASILICA DI SANTA CECILIA IN TRASTEVERE

VIA ROMA LIBERA

ELVIS LIVES

TRASTEVERE/ MASTAI

Piazza Mastai

ANICIA

Piazza di Santa Cecilia

VERSO SUD

LE LEVAIN

San Cosimato

VIA DI

VIALE A RIPA

VIA DELLA LUCE

MUNICIPIO I

VIA EMILIO MOROSINI

VIA

VIA DI SAN MICHELE

TRASTEVERE/ MIN. P. ISTRUZIONE

INDUNO

CHIESA DI SAN FRANCESCO D'ASSISI A RIPA GRANDE

LUNGOTEVERE PORTO DI RIPA GRANDE

Teatro Trastevere

VIALE DI TRASTEVERE

N

0   100 m

(River   Tiber)

LUNGOTEVERE AVENTINO

Nuovo Sacher (cinema)

VIALE DELLE MURA PORTUENSI

Mercato di Porta Portese

PONTE SUBLICIO

LUNGOTEVERE TESTACCIO

TRASTEVERE/ BERNARD. DA FELTRE

EMPORIO

Parco di San Alessio

VILLA DEL PRIORATA DI MALTA

TO FERNANDA & OFF-ROMA (SEE MAP LEFT)

VIA BENEDETTO MUSOLINO

CLIVO PORTUENSE

VIA PORTUENSE

Fiume Tevere

Chiesa di Sant'Anselmo all'Aventino

ANTICA CACIARA TRASTEVERINA

Via di San Francesco a Ripa 140A/B

06 581 2815

www.anticacaciara.it/antica_caciara.html

Open Mon–Sat 7.30am–8pm

Not so much a deli as an institution, Antica Caciara Trasteverina has been whetting appetites since 1900. Owner Roberto Polica knows his regulars by name, not to mention the many artisan producers who stock his heavenly store. It's best known for its ricotta di pecora (sheep's milk ricotta), which arrives fresh each morning from just outside the city. It's commonly sold out by lunch – savvy locals head in at opening during festive periods to ensure their share. If you're a fan of burrata cheese, turn up on Friday mornings for the week's super-fresh delivery. Roberto's Umbrian roots are reflected in the fine selection of salumi (cured meats) from the central Italian region. Pull yourself away only to drool over tubs of acciughe salate (salted anchovies), olive nere secche al forno (oven-dried black olives), porcini mushrooms and barrels laden with bottles of wine. If you're famished and it's not too busy, they'll even make you a panino with fresh local bread.

LOCAL TIP

Much-loved no-frills Bar San Calisto (Piazza San Calisto 3) pours well-priced drinks: try the Sambuca con la mosca (Sambuca with coffee beans).

VERSO SUD

Piazza di Santa Cecilia 16
06 5833 3668
Open Mon–Sat
10.30am–7.30pm

Women with a weakness for elegant yet edgy style adore Verso Sud, an independent showcase for harder-to-find, cognoscenti designers. Look for Italy's Ter Et Bantine and conceptualist Sara Lanzi; Barcelona's Laura B; Antwerp's Christian Wijnants and Paris-based Jerome Dreyfuss and Véronique Leroy. It's the only place in town to stock Belgian-born designer Cédric Charlier. The list of labels is refreshed each season by on-point owner Ornella de Falco. Accessories include artisan Italian millinery and high-end handmade footwear from names like Marsell, Roberto Del Carlo, Alberto Fasciani and Rocco P. Last-season stock is sold at slashed prices in the basement. Freshly minted threads aside, the space also hosts a collection of vintage fashion, curated by co-owner Valentina Stefani. On any given visit you could land a pair of well-preserved Jimmy Choo heels, a YSL handbag or a Miu Miu cocktail dress. It's a hit with local filmmakers, who flick through the racks in search of unique, camera-friendly outfits.

3.

MARTA RAY
Via del Moro 6
06 581 1108
www.martaray.it
Open Mon–Sun 10am–8pm

Polish-born local designer
Marta Anna Ratajczak
continues to win fans with her
fetching handmade leather
bags and shoes. The ballet
flats are a huge hit, with more
than 50 shades, memory-foam
inner soles, and the choice
of a round or pointed toe.
You'll also find cool boots and
summer sandals, all created
using Italian leather. Marta
Ray's bags are the bomb,
fusing contemporary styling
with clever functionality.
You might score a bag that
divides into two, or one with
changeable dimensions.
Styles include clutches,
handbags, totes, backpacks
and overnight bags, while the
range of unisex accessories
includes wallets, purses and
origami-inspired coin purses,
as well as cardholders and
tassel-leather keyrings. Up-
and-coming plans include
a collection of sunglasses
in bag-matching hues
and a brand-new range
of men's bags and kicks.
Rejoice! This store is the
original, with another two
branches in Rome and one
in Florence.

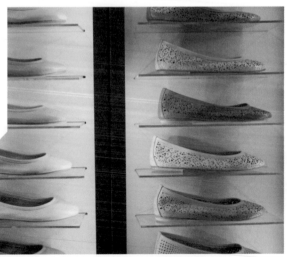

4.

ELVIS LIVES

Via di San Francesco a Ripa 27
06 4550 9543
www.elvislives.it
Open Mon–Sat 10.30am–2pm
& 3.30–8pm

Elvis is alive, well and trading in Trastevere. This kooky hipster providore has all bases covered: ironic tees and totes, instant cameras, reissued classic-rock LPs from the likes of Iggy Pop and Joy Divison, and even collectable TV and movie figurines. It's the passion project of mates Marco Polica and Marco Macciocca, who met working as graphic designers in the fashion industry before starting their own t-shirt printing business. The tees – made using ethically produced organic cotton – bemuse with tongue-in-cheek slogans like 'Delete Browser History', Roman slang and the shop's own logo, a depiction of Elvis as Christ. The guys also produce their own range of quality chinos, sold alongside Komono eyewear, Herschel wallets and backpacks, and playful Barbosa watches. The store attracts no shortage of Gen-Y and millennial customers with its cool collection of cult-status instant cameras from Lomography, a Vienna-based outfit dedicated to analogue, experimental and creative photography.

5.

OFF–ROMA
Via Giovanni da
Castel Bolognese 75
06 580 9108
Open Mon–Sat 10am–8pm
(closed 2–4pm Jun–mid-Aug)

Hidden away on a nondescript side street, OFF-Roma bursts with eclectic homewares, accessories and furniture, both new, old and upcycled. Scour the space for anything from hand-painted ceramic bowls from southern Italy to painted concrete tiles from Morocco, colourful drinking glasses, old bakery trays and quirky table lamps. It's heaven for those who prefer their interiors with a twist of the bohemian, the industrial or the plain quirky. The space is run by architect Barbara Giovinazzo, her artistic sister Simona, their interior-designer mother Laura Giardello and Laura's partner, Bruno Correnti. Bruno uses salvaged timber, metal and other materials to make rustic, one-off furniture pieces, while pre-existing pieces like chairs might get a revamp using fresh, bold upholstery. The upcycling motif extends to other items in-store, such as idiosyncratic bags and jewellery made locally using men's neckties. The store also stocks Italian and English textiles and wallpaper.

LOCAL TIP
Follow your nose to heavenly scented Biscottificio Innocenti (Via della Luce 21), a family-run biscuit factory operating since the 1940s.

LE LEVAIN

Via Luigi Santini 22
06 6456 2880
www.lelevainroma.it
Open Mon–Sat 8am–8.30pm,
Sun 9am–6.30pm

A petite slice of Paris in Trastevere? Très bon! Compact, artisanal Le Levain – decked out with a handful of benches and bar tables – peddles some of the city's best croissants, made fresh behind a great glass wall. We're talking flaky, fluffy creations with a slightly salty taste good enough to draw the French themselves. I drool at the mere thought of the pain au chocolat and pain aux raisins, both equally fine ways to start the day. Not that it's all rich, sweet, buttery recklessness here. Savoury options include freshly made panini farciti (hamburger-style panini), baguettes filled with fresh green leaves, and mini quiches. The piatto del giorno (plate of the day) might see you noshing on a vibrant salad of beef tartare, zucchini, confit tomatoes, Parmigiano-Reggiano and balsamic vinegar…always best followed by a pretty pastel-coloured macaron. Although the coffee comes out of a vending machine, it's surprisingly inoffensive. Wi-fi is available, as well as a small selection of craft beer.

7.

DA ENZO

Via dei Vascellari 29
06 581 2260
www.daenzoal29.com
Open Mon–Sat 12.30–3pm
& 7.30–11pm (closed 3 weeks
in Aug)

Queues are the norm at
this small, casual bastion of
home-cooking, run by affable
siblings Chiara, Francesco
and Roberto. It's like the
Roman nonna (grandmother)
you never had, serving up
culinary hugs in the form of
simple, scrumptious Roman
dishes. While the menu
names all the ubiquitous
standards (carbonara, we're
looking at you), it offers more
variety than many other
trattorias in town. Seasonal
daily specials may include
sublime zuppa di cavolo nero
e patate (black cabbage and
potato soup). Ingredients are
sourced from smaller local
producers, including organic
olive oil from northern Lazio
and artisanal dry pastas
from Lazio and neighbouring
Abruzzo. The egg-based
pasta fresca (fresh pasta) is
made in-house. There's a
degustation of various olive
oils to try, and carnivores
shouldn't miss the pork-
and-beef polpette al sugo
(meatballs in sauce), best
washed down with a glass
of local red. Lunch is a no-
reservations affair, so go early
(Tuesdays and Wednesdays
are usually quietest) or
prepare to wait.

8.

FERNANDA

Via Crescenzo del Monte 18
347 4459593
www.osteriafernanda.com
Open Mon–Tues 7.30–11pm,
Wed–Sat 12.30–2.30pm &
7.30–11pm

Light-washed, split-level
Fernanda delivers bold
culinary statements off the
main tourist track. A large
glass pane into the kitchen
reveals a young, gung-ho
team, led by head chef
Davide Del Duca. A deep
passion for all things earthy
and experimental drives his
intriguing dishes, such as
yolk-filled ravioli served with
pecorino cream, cardoncelli
mushrooms and a broth of
roots and toasted dry fruits.
Davide's other obsession
is fermentation, which
may see tender moulard
duck paired with hazelnut
paste and fermented-plum
gel. The complimentary
welcome snacks are always
a bite-sized thrill, whether
chicken liver with green
curry, clarified butter and
mandarin gel, or a 'cannolo'
of celery and broccoli rabe
(a bitter green) spiked with
trumpet-mushroom powder.
While not all dishes smash it,
overall quality is high, with
degustation menus priced a
little lower than many other
contemporary fine-dining
hotspots. Bookings are a
sensible idea, especially for
dinner or Saturday lunch.

7.

7.

8.

8.

8.

7.

9.

ALEMBIC
Piazza in Piscinula 51
06 580 0681
www.alembic.it
Open Mon–Sun
10.30am–1.30am

An unmarked corner bar, restaurant and art gallery in one, Alembic takes its name from an ancient distillation instrument. While the interior includes a tilting column or two, the look here is more atelier than lab: lush potted palms, old chandeliers, flickering candles and fashionably distressed vintage furniture. It's a sultry headiness that draws emerging artists and actors, not to mention the odd superstar: is that Ben Stiller? Probably. Jars of fresh chillies and rosemary adorn the concrete bar, where well-mixed libations include a blissful gin and tonic spiked with smoked rosemary and juniper berries. For the peckish, fresh and interesting appetisers may include eggplant rolls filled with vegetable cream and pesto, ceviche, tacos, burger mignon and salads. The evening aperitivo is good value, with a spread that usually includes pasta and fresh vegetables. If you like your drinks with a side of live tunes, head in for live music several times a week in the cooler months.

ENOTECA FERRARA

Piazza Trilussa 4
06 5833 3920
www.enotecaferrara.it
Open Mon–Sun 6pm–2am
(closed Sun in Aug)

LOCAL TIP
For a thirst-quenching
selection of craft beer
and fine wood-fired pizza,
dive into perennially
popular Bir & Fud
(Via Benedetta 23).

Ferrara is where trasteverini (Trastevere locals) go for a decent aperitivo (pre-dinner drinks and nibbles). It's an intimate, convivial spot: timber-beamed ceilings, wooden floorboards and a democratic soundtrack spanning Johnny Cash to Pearl Jam. The affable Andrea is usually behind the bar, a wine aficionado happy to steer you towards the perfect drop. Expect around 24 Italian wines by the glass, including more unusual offerings from lesser known winemakers.

The evening aperitivo spread is one of Rome's most generous, with bites such as riso nero con polpo (black rice with octopus), inventive salads, pizza topped with smoked provola cheese, börek pastries, and dangerously addictive gnocco fritto (deep-fried pillows of pizza dough). Blackboard offerings include boards of cured meats and cheeses, with a focus on smaller artisanal producers. There's an adjacent osteria and restaurant, though the abundant aperitivo usually ends up becoming dinner.

Culture vultures are especially spoiled in Trastevere's northern reaches. The former home of Queen Christina of Sweden is now **Galleria Corsini** (Via della Lungara 10), home to a chunk of Italy's national art collection. This includes Caravaggio's *San Giovanni Battista* (St John the Baptist), as well as works by Rubens, de Ribera and Guercino.

Across the street, Renaissance **Villa Farnesina** (Via della Lungara 230) is lavished with frescoes, some attributed to Raphael.

If you need to clear your mind, take refuge in the **Orto Botanico** (Largo Cristina di Svezia 24), a 30-acre botanical garden directly behind Palazzo Corsini. The garden creeps up the slope of **Gianicolo Hill**, whose summit terrace offers a prime view of the city. To reach the terrace, you'll need to head up Passeggiata del Gianicolo as there is no direct access from the Orto Botanico.

Gianicolo Hill is also home to the **Chiesa di San Pietro in Montorio** (Piazza San Pietro in Montorio 2). The church's courtyard is home to Donato Bramante's early 16th-century **Tempietto**, one of the first and finest achievements of the High Renaissance. The circular temple reputedly occupies the very spot where St Peter was martyred.

Back in Trastevere proper is the **Basilica di Santa Maria in Trastevere** (Piazza Santa Maria in Trastevere), a largely Romanesque church with 3rd-century roots, a Baroque portico and dazzling 12th- and 13th-century mosaics, some by Pietro Cavallini.

Cavallini is also responsible for the beautiful nun's choir fresco in the convent flanking the **Basilica di Santa Cecilia in Trastevere** (Piazza di Santa Cecilia) further east. The fresco is accessible between 10am and 12.30pm Monday to Saturday and from 11.30am to 12.30pm on Sundays. In the basilica itself is a late-Renaissance sculpture by Stefano Maderno depicting St Cecilia's miraculously preserved body. The saint's remains were discovered at the **Catacombe di San Callisto** on Rome's Appian Way almost 14 centuries after her death circa 230 CE.

Catholic legend also weighs heavily at nearby **Chiesa di San Francesco d'Assisi a Ripa Grande** (Piazza di San Francesco d'Assisi 88). It's said that St Francis crashed here in 1219, and the saint's cell (accessible in the afternoons if the curator is on-site) houses his crucifix and the rock he purportedly used as a pillow. The church's more exuberant claim to fame is Gian Lorenzo Bernini's sexually charged sculpture of Franciscan nun Ludovica Albertoni.

RANSOM
& CO

CACIO
E PEPE

VIA RUFFINI

VIA LUIGI

VIA SETTEMBRINI

⊠

SETTEMBRINI

Piazza dei
Martiri di
Belfiore

VIA NICOLA RICCIOTTI

VIA FEDERICO CONFALONIERI

VIA AVEZZANA

VIA GIUSEPPE

Giuseppe
Avezzana
Apartment

MILIZIE

TO
MAP RIGHT
(ALONG VIALE
DELLE MILIZIE)

VIALE DELLE

Ⓜ LEPANTO

PRATI

It may be named for the marshy prati (fields) that stood here until the late 19th century, but modern Prati is a sophisticated creature. Broad, tree-lined avenues and elegant turn-of-the-century palazzi (large buildings) set a very bourgeois scene.

Home to the Supreme Court and main headquarters of Italy's public national broadcaster, RAI, its on-point restaurants throng with lawyers, journalists and TV producers. Respectable locals saunter between department stores, boutiques and delis on and off Via Cola di Rienzo, the neighbourhood's energetic spine. Come evening, ties are loosened and Prati's sophisticated bars buzz with a fashionable, predominately Italian crowd, contrasting sharply with its tourist-heavy neighbour, the Vatican.

24   JUN 8016

SHOP
1 RECHICLE
2 RANSOM & CO
3 IL SELLAIO SERAFINI
   PELLETTERIA

EAT
4 CACIO E PEPE
5 PIZZARIUM
6 TED

EAT AND DRINK
7 SETTEMBRINI
8 LA COMPAGNIA DEL PANE
9 IL SORPASSO
10 LA ZANZARA

DRINK
11 SCIASCIA CAFFÈ

Teatro
dell'Angelo

Relais
San Pietro

VIA TRIONFALE

VIALE DELLE MILIZIE

VIA OTRANTO

VIA BARLETTA

MILIZIE/
ANGELICO

TO
CACIO E PEPE,
SETTEMBRINI &
RANSOM & CO
(SEE MAP LEFT)

CESARE

VIALE GIULIO

SCIASCIA
CAFFÈ

New Design
St Peter Hotel

VIA LEONE IV

VIA FAMAGOSTA

VIA OSTIA

OTTAVIANO

VIALE GIULIO CESARE

LA COMPAGNIA
DEL PANE

OTTAVIANO

Maison
Candia
Luxury
House

VIA CANDIA

TO
PIZZARIUM
(NOT SHOWN ON MAP)

ANTICA
MANIFATTURA
CAPPELLI

Teatro
Prati

IL SELLAIO
SERAFINI
PELLETTERIA

VIA CAIO MARIO

VIA FABIO MASSIMO

Tango
Hotel

Azzurro
Scipioni
(cinema)

Hotel
Amalia

GERMANICO

RECHICLE

GRACCHI

VIA VESPASIANO

VIA

VIA OTTAVIANO

PRATI
RIONE XXII

VIALE VATICANO

VIA DEI

VIA COLA DI RIENZO

MUSEO
PIO-CLEMENTINO

Grand Hotel
Olympic

Vatican
Museums

Necropoli
della via
Triumphalis

Piazza del
Risorgimento

MUNICIPIO I

TED

STRADONE DEI GIARDINI

Cortile
della
Pigna

LA ZANZARA

RISORGIMENTO/
S. PIETRO

Residenza
Crescenzio

VIA

CRESCENZIO

CITTÀ DEL
VATICANO

BORGO

VIA STEFANO

ANGELICO

VIA MASCHERINO

IL SORPASSO

PORCARI

Cortile del
Belvedere

BORGO

VITTORIO

VIA PLAUTO

Hotel
Atlante
Star

VIA DI BELVEDERE

Cortile dei
Falegnami

Cortile
d'Onore

Piazza
della
Città
Leonina

Hotel
Sant'Anna

BORGO

Hotel della
Conciliazione

VIA DI PORTA ANGELICA

VIA DEL

VIA

PIO

Palazzo
Apostolico

BORGO SANT'ANGELO

VIA DI PORTA CASTELLO

SISTINE
CHAPEL

Cortile
di San
Damaso

BORGO
RIONE XIV

CHORUS
CAFÉ

San Paolo

VIA DEI

CORRIDORI

St Peter's
Basilica

Piazza
San Pietro

VIA DELLA CONCILIAZIONE

San Pietro

VIA DELLA

CONCILIAZIONE

Columbus
Hotel

BORGO

SANTO

SPIRITO

LUNGOTEVERE IN SASSIA

Chiesa di
Santo
Spirito
in Sassia

Piazza del
Sant'Uffizio

Ordine di
Sant'Agostino

N

Curia
Generalizia
dei
Gesuiti

GALLERIA PRINCIPE AMEDEO SAVOIA- AOSTA

0   100 m

1.

RECHICLE
Piazza dell'Unità 21
06 3265 2469
Open Mon–Sat 10.30am–2pm
& 3.30–7pm

Fashionistas with more style than euros will fall head over heels for this consignment store. Last-season threads and accessories arrive each day from fickle style-lovers (and the occasional Italian star), and are given the critical once-over by owner Anna Lisa Martella. Only the best items are chosen for the store, whether it's an electric-purple Thierry Mugler jacket, fur-lined Celine stilettos, or must-have handbags from Chanel, Stella McCartney and Jimmy Choo. From the coats and suits, to the dresses and heels, the stock is in mint condition – some items still have the original tags attached. Prices are a steal compared to their original value: a Valentino cashmere suit can go for €200; an embroidered silk Alberta Ferretti dress for €120; a Tiffany necklace and bracelet for €350. Anything still unsold on the racks after two months is slashed by 50%. Fans of vintage can usually find extraordinary throwbacks from the 1950s to the 1970s, too. Haute heaven.

2.

LOCAL TIP

Milliner Patrizia Fabri offers ready-to-wear and made-to-measure hats for men and women at her atelier Antica Manifattura Cappelli (Via degli Scipioni 46).

RANSOM & CO

Via Giuseppe Avezzana 25
06 320 0468
www.ransomclothing.it
Open Mon–Sat 11am–7pm

Ransom & CO is a rarity in Rome: an independent store selling cool, locally designed men's threads that are both affordable and well made. Co-owners Alessandro and Andrea source quality fabrics for their handsome preppy, smart-casual range of graphic tees, 'worn in' Oxford shirts, jumpers, cardigans, blazers and outerwear with interesting detailing and subtle twists. I also love their stretch corduroy and chino pants, which retail for less than €70. Expect mostly solid, muted colours, as well as international accessories such as attention-seeking Scandi socks, Canadian backpacks and Belgian glasses and watches. The back of the store has a smaller selection of fun, relaxed women's fashion from Danish brand Only.

3.

IL SELLAIO SERAFINI PELLETTERIA

Via Caio Mario 14
06 321 1719
www.serafinipelletteria.it
Open Mon–Fri 9.30am–
7.30pm, Sat 9.30am–1pm &
3.30–7.30pm

In business for more than 70 years, Signor Ferruccio Serafini is one of only a few genuine leatherwork artisans remaining in Rome today. His seasoned hands craft beautiful, classic bags for women and men, among them briefcases, duffle bags and backpacks, shoulder bags, tablet satchels and laptop cases. Bespoke bags take one to three weeks and can be freighted abroad. Male feet get an instant upgrade with his esteemed brogues and moccasins; the mocassina alla Marlon (Marlon moccasin) – popular with Prati's avvocati (lawyers) – is named after its most famous fan, Marlon Brando. The range of accessories includes leather belts, wallets, coin trays and pencil holders, all made using top-quality leather from Tuscany's Lo Stivale tannery. Expect to pay €40 to €50 for a belt, around €50 for a wallet, €180 to €220 for shoes, and between €110 and €450 for a bag, depending on size and style. Signor Serafini also repairs bags and suitcases (usually two to three days).

4.

CACIO E PEPE

Via Giuseppe Avezzana 11
06 321 7268
www.trattoriacacioepepeprati.
com
Open Mon–Fri 12.30–3.15pm
& 7.30–11.30pm, Sat
12.30–3.15pm

At a press conference in Rome, Canadian singer-songwriter Alanis Morissette took out a piece of paper and asked for directions to this humble, convivial spot. Other VIP fans have included the late American chef and TV food guru Anthony Bourdain, who tucked into the trattoria's eponymous pasta dish. The cacio e pepe (pasta with Parmigiano-Reggiano and pecorino romano cheeses and cracked pepper) here is usually smashing, but it does have competition from the carbonara (pasta with egg, parmesan and guanciale – cured pig's cheek). Charismatic owner Gianni – whose parents opened the place back in 1964 – will proudly tell you his pasta is freshly made each day. If you're not in a pasta mood, look out for melanzane alla parmigiana (eggplant parmigiana) or the equally comforting polpette (meatballs), usually offered al sugo (in a tomato-based sauce) or al limone (with lemon). Seating is mostly alfresco, mercifully covered and heated in the cooler months. Consider calling ahead; it's that popular.

3.

4.

3.

5.

PIZZARIUM

Via della Meloria 43
06 3974 5416
Open Mon–Sun 11am–10pm

Pizzarium is the Holy Grail for pizza al taglio (pizza by the slice) fans; its founder – pizzaiolo (pizza maker) Gabriele Bonci – is famously nicknamed the 'Michelangelo of dough'. Bonci and his team use only cold-fermented, heirloom-wheat-based dough for their bases, which are risen for 72 hours and baked thrice for a perfect consistency. Toppings are seasonal, regional and artisanal. Scan the counter for the day's dizzying array of offerings, a mixture of signatures like tomato and oregano and rotating combos like broccoletti with taleggio cheese, provola cheese with pancetta, or zucchini flowers paired with ricotta and anchovies. If you're into your spice, look out for 'nduja, a spreadable salami from Calabria made with pork, roasted peppers and spices. To order, grab a number and wait your turn at the counter. Next take your receipt to the register to pay. Head back to the counter and wait for your order to be called. Seating is limited to a few benches outside, so prepare to eat standing.

6.

TED

Via Terenzio 12–16
06 9451 7168
http://tedlobsterburger.it
Open Sun–Thurs 9am–1am,
Fri–Sat 9am–2am

Lobster rolls, burgers and cocktails make for an unholy trinity at TED, a polished New York–style bistro with prerequisite Edison bulbs, industrial accents, showpiece bar and bustling open kitchen. The grilled lobster rolls are decadent and satisfying, though a little lighter on the butter than those served in the US. Burgers are equally succulent, made with soft brioche buns and served with fries. If you're doing penance, healthier options include salads and a daily soup. For local flavour, there are specials such as polpette di melanzane (eggplant 'meat balls'), while those hankering for a little Mexican can dig into generous tacos (one serve should suffice most appetites). Despite the American-centric menu, the crowd is mostly Roman, from lunching shoppers to Prati business types.

7.

SETTEMBRINI

Via Luigi Settembrini 21
06 9761 0325
http://viasettembrini.com
Open Mon–Sun 7am–1.30am

Within strutting distance of RAI's TV headquarters, this contemporary, cultured cafe-bistro is a great place to star-spot Italian celebrities. It's as good for a morning cappuccino as it is for a quick panino, power lunch, see-and-be-seen aperitivo (pre-dinner drinks and nibbles) or lingering dinner. From bread and pastries to gelato, much of what's on offer is made from scratch in-house and is dictated by seasonality. The fish is always local; the cheeses are from little-known producers; and daily specials are guided by what's available from farmers. Flavours are sophisticated Italian, whether a simple panino of tuna, sautéed wild chicory and candied lemon; gnocchi with smoked pumpkin and cinnamon; or duck paired with endive, grapefruit and pine-nut 'milk'. The cellar – home to around 200 wines – can be booked for private dinners, and a busy calendar of events presents young Calabrian winemakers and bloody-Mary-making artisan tomato growers.

7.

6.

7.

7.

6.

8

LA COMPAGNIA DEL PANE

Via Fabio Massimo 89
06 324 1605
www.compagniadelpane.it
Open Mon–Sat 7am–9pm

Third-generation 'The Bread Company' wears many hats: artisan bakery and pastry shop, gourmet deli, bar and casual eatery. Locals and office workers head in through the day for early morning cappuccinos and still-warm ciambellone (Italian ring cake), sit-down lunches, or pre-dinner spritz. The coffee – from small Florentine roaster Piansa – is one of my favourites in town. From the cornetti (Italian croissants), biscotti and pastries, to the crisp pizza, everything is made fresh, right below you in CDP's sprawling lab. Come lunch, workers tuck into staples like saltimbocca alla romana (veal escalope with sage and prosciutto) or seasonal dishes from carciofi alla romana (Roman-style artichokes) to nourishing zuppe (soups). The common thread is top-notch ingredients, from the olive oil and pasta, to the fresh produce itself. It's worth scanning the deli counter for take-home goods such as soft, gooey stracchino cheese from far-northern Piedmont and prosciutto di Parma from artisan producer Pio Tosini.

9.

IL SORPASSO

Via Properzio 31–33
06 8902 4554
http://sorpasso.info
Open Mon–Fri 7.30am–1am,
Sat 9am–1am

A studious mishmash of recycled timber, subway tiles and suspended prosciutti, Il Sorpasso is a huge hit with the fashionable Prati set for morning coffee and juices, lunchtime salads and pasta, aperitivo, dinner or a night cap. Notable edibles include the trapazzini (pyramid-shaped stuffed pizza) and the selection of salumi (cured meats) and formaggi (cheeses), the latter perfect for a vino and people-watching session. The best time for this is during aperitivo, when the loyal crowd spills out onto the street, sipping, chatting, flirting and grazing on complimentary morsels offered by affable roving waiters. Chances are affable owner Paul Pansera is in the crowd; that's him in the paste-up to the right of the entrance. If you're after a quiet dinner, this is *not* the place for you. The cellar shelves around 500 mostly Italian wines; there are decent choices by the glass, as well as well-crafted cocktails.

10.

LA ZANZARA

Via Crescenzio 84
06 6839 2227
www.lazanzararoma.com
Open Mon–Fri 7.30am–2am,
Sat–Sun 8am–2am

White subway tiles, industrial lights and a cocktail list scribbled on vintage mirrors: it's a case of New York meets Paris at La Zanzara (The Mosquito), a buzzing, sprawling bar and bistro. Best seats in the house are at the retro-inspired bar, where suspender-strapped barkeeps stir, shake and pour libations with names like Soho, Root's Sailor #2, Drive In and Tiki Tuka. The back bar is a well-stocked beast, with an interesting selection of whiskey and gin; if you're into G&T, opt for Roby Marton gin from north-eastern Italy. Food options span morning eggs, pastries and pancakes, to eat-and-go panini, and more substantial pastas, soups and grilled meats. Fortes, though, are the cocktails and deli bites, the latter including Spanish jamon (ham), pistachio-speckled mortadella (sausage) and fresh mozzarella. After all, your focus should be on the bar and the eligible Prati crowd, peppered with no shortage of dashing professionals wanting to forget the pressures of the day.

11.

SCIASCIA CAFFÈ

Via Fabio Massimo 80A
06 321 1580
http://sciasciacaffe1919.it
Open Mon–Sun 7am–9pm

For a dose of nostalgia, slip into this 1919 Prati senior. The bar is in the backroom, a snug hideaway graced with wooden and mirrored panels, vintage photographs of the neighbourhood, and charming vested barstaff. Faithful regulars swear you'll get one of the best cappuccinos in the city here, made using the cafe's own house-roasted beans. While the cappuccino is perfectly acceptable, Sciascia's strength in my opinion is its inimitable caffè con cioccolato (espresso with chocolate). Watch as the barkeep pours thick melted dark chocolate into your delicate porcelain cup, artfully coating the sides before adding the espresso. The result is a beautiful hit of coffee and chocolate that's nuanced and not too sweet. Later in the day, the place is also an atmospheric spot for a pre-dinner tipple. Don't forget to scan the shelves in the front room for take-home artisanal chocolates, vintage-style tins of liquorice and mints, and roasted coffee beans.

LOCAL TIP
Marble-clad Chorus Café
(Via della Conciliazione 4)
is a hit with Prati's
beautiful people for its
smooth cocktails and
Manhattan-esque style.

Prati skirts a string of unmissable sights. Top billing goes to **St Peter's Basilica** (Piazza San Pietro), the largest and most impressive basilica in Italy. Consecrated in 1626, the current building took more than a century to complete, its succession of architects including Donato Bramante, Michelangelo, Giacomo della Porta, Domenico Fontana and Carlo Maderno. Michelangelo designed its famous dome and sculpted its deeply moving *Pietà*, an image of the Virgin Mary holding the body of Christ, the only sculpture the artist ever signed. The latter is kept in fine company by Gian Lorenzo Bernini's bronze baldachin (canopy), which soars above the papal altar. Bernini also designed the basilica's monumental square, the **Piazza San Pietro**.

Free English-language tours of the basilica run on weekdays from October to late May. Queues at St Peter's Basilica are usually shorter at lunch and in the late afternoon. Shorts, sleeveless tops and miniskirts are prohibited. For a heavenly view of Rome, tackle the 551 steps (320 steps if you cheat by also using the lift) that take you up to the dome; access to the stairs is to the right of the basilica's main portico.

To the north of St Peter's, the **Vatican Museums** (Viale Vaticano) is where you'll find the **Sistine Chapel** and its astounding frescoes that are the work of a who's who of Renaissance talent including Michelangelo, Botticelli, Giotto, Fra Angelico, Titian, Caravaggio, Leonardo da Vinci and Perugino. Other must-sees at the Vatican Museums include the **Museo Pio-Clementino** – famed for its classical sculptures and double-helix staircase – and the **Pinacoteca**, whose masterpieces include Raphael's swansong, *La Trasfigurazione* (The Transfiguration). The distinctive brushstrokes of both Perugino and Raphael adorn the so-called **Stanze di Raffaello** (Rooms of Raphael), four frescoed chambers that formed part of Pope Julius II's private apartments in the early 16th century.

You'll need to book at least a week ahead to wander through the spirit-lifting **Vatican Gardens**; accessible only on a two-hour guided tour.

From Piazza San Pietro, Mussolini's Via della Conciliazione shoots eastward to brawny riverfront **Castel Sant'Angelo** (Lungotevere Castello 50). The castle has played numerous roles over the last two millennia; it was initially built as a mausoleum for Roman emperor Hadrian and has also served as a medieval papal fortress. It's now armed with paintings, sculpture, historic firearms and sweeping views from its panoramic terrace.

Connecting the castle to Rome's centro storico (historic centre) is the unapologetically romantic 2nd-century **Ponte Sant'Angelo**, the bridge's elegant 17th-century angels a creation of the irrepressible Bernini.

Toil, calcio (football) and offal have long defined Testaccio, a left-leaning, working-class enclave flanked by Aventine Hill and the Tiber. This is the historic home of football team A.S. Roma and the city's quarto quinto (offal) dishes, the latter served in what are some of Rome's most authentic and revered trattorias and restaurants. Such carnivorous leanings hark back to the days when Testaccio housed the city's slaughterhouse.

These days, weathered pensionati (pensioners) and earthy pizzaioli (pizza makers) rub shoulders with a growing number of filmmakers, artists and designers, all drawn to Testaccio's cult-status eateries, pumping nightlife and enduring come-as-you-are attitude.

GIANICOLENSE
QUARTIERE XII

VIALE DI TRASTEVERE
MUSOLINO
BENEDETTO
VIA
VIA DEGLI ORTI DI TRASTEVERE
CLIVO
PORTUENSE
VIA ANGELO BARGONI
PORTUENSE
VIA
Fiume Tevere

TESTACCIO

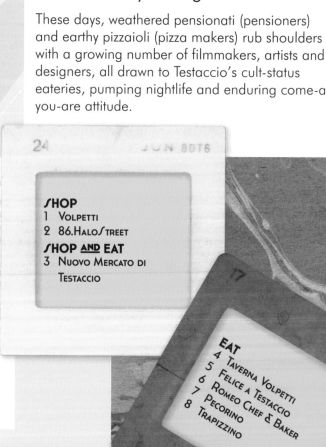

24   JUN 8076

SHOP
1 VOLPETTI
2 86.HaloStreet
SHOP AND EAT
3 NUOVO MERCATO DI
   TESTACCIO

17

EAT
4 TAVERNA VOLPETTI
5 FELICE A TESTACCIO
6 ROMEO CHEF & BAKER
7 PECORINO
8 TRAPIZZINO

PONTE
SUBLICIO

Parco di San Alessio
VILLA DEL
PRIORATA
DI MALTA

*Piazza dei
Cavalieri
di Malta*

EMPORIO

*Piazza
dell'Emporio*

Fiume Tevere (River Tiber)

**ROMEO
CHEF &
BAKER**

*Chiesa di
Sant'Anselmo
all'Aventino*

**RIPA
RIONE XII**

TESTACCIO

VIA ANTONIO

LUNGOTEVERE

VIA ROMOLO

VIA GUSTAVO

CECCHI

VESPUCCI

GESSI

BRANCA

MARMORATA

VIA PIETRO QUERINI

MARMORATA/
VANVITELLI

AMERIGO

BIANCHI

VIA GIOVANNI

VANVITELLI

VIA

VIA

LUIGI

VIA LUCA

*Teatro
Petrolini*

RUBATTINO

PIAZZA DI SANTA MARIA LIBERATRICE

*Giardino
Famigliadi
Consiglio*

VIA

MASTRO

86.HALOSTREET

TRAPIZZINO

*Teatro
Vittoria*

*Chiesa di
Santa Maria
Liberatrice*

VIA

GIORGIO

*Piazza
Testaccio*

DELLA

**L'OASI
DELLA
BIRRA**

MANUZIO

ALDO

ROBBIA

VOLPETTI

*Greenwich
(cinema)*

NICOLA

**TESTACCIO
RIONE XX**

VIA

TAVERNA VOLPETTI

MARMORATA/
GALVANI

VIA GIOVANNI BATTISTA BODONI

MANUZIO

ZABAGLIA

GINORI

**FELICE A
TESTACCIO**

VIA

ALDO

LORENZO GHIBERTI

VOLTA

GALVANI

VIA

VIA ALESSANDRO

VIA

N

**NUOVO
MERCATO DI
TESTACCIO**

VIA BENIAMINO FRANKLIN

MUNICIPIO I

*Hotel
Re Testa*

GALVANI

VIA

VIA NICOLA ZABAGLIA

*Teatro di
Documenti*

0   100 m

PECORINO

FLAVIO AL
VELAVEVODETTO

Mattatoio

MONTE TESTACCIO
(MONTE DEI COCCI)

1.

VOLPETTI

Via Marmorata 47
06 574 2352
www.volpetti.com
Open Mon–Wed 8.30am–2pm
& 4.30–8.30pm, Thurs–Sat
8.30am–8.30pm

Drooling is practically
mandatory at Volpetti. One
of Rome's most revered
gourmet delis, this culinary
cave is packed with cured
meats, an impressive variety
of cheeses, rustic sausages,
plump olives, dried porcini
mushrooms, marinated
vegetables and jar upon jar of
mouthwatering condiments.
It's one of my staples for fresh
buffalo-milk mozzarella and I
usually also leave with a jar of
the mostarda di Cremona, a
bitter-sweet northern-Italian
condiment made of candied
fruit immersed in mustard-oil
flavoured syrup. Although
prices are generally higher
here, the products are among
the best you'll find in the
city. Easy take-home treats
include artisan olive oils and
vinegars, as well as harder-
to-find products like white
truffle honey (yes, there is
such a thing). Another plus
is the gracious, helpful staff.
The deli also serves a few
ready-to-eat bites.

LOCAL TIPS

It's worth following
your deli visit with
lunch or dinner at
Volpetti's sit-down
eatery just around
the corner (Via
Alessandro Volta 8).

Seasonal garden
bar Tram Depot (Via
Marmorata 13) serves
speciality coffee,
juices and liquor
from a vintage 1903
tram carriage.

86.HALOSTREET

Via G. B. Bodoni 8
www.86halostreet.com
Open Mon 3.30–7.30pm,
Tues–Sat 10.30am–1.30pm &
3.30–7.30pm

Young designers Agnese Consorsi and Francesca Metta design and sew women's threads, and intermittently entertain friends in their little white atelier. The name is an amalgamation of their birth year and the halos associated with one of their muses, the late American artist Jean-Michel Basquiat. Other inspirations for their designs include observations of daily life; even the detail in a local fountain could spark an idea. What makes their work unique is the merging of Italian sartorial traditions with strong, contemporary graphics and high-tech fabrics, from tencel and vinyl to scuba (a neoprene-like material). The result is next-gen 'Made in Italy' pieces with often edgy, deconstructed or playful silhouettes. Adding to this, only a small amount of each fabric is bought, ensuring creations are either limited edition or one-offs. Accessories are restricted to the duo's cool shopping bag, with can be used as a tote.

NUOVO MERCATO DI TESTACCIO

Via Beniamino Franklin
www.mercatoditestaccio.it
Open Mon–Sat 7am–3.30pm

Traditionalists pine for the neighbourhood's old market, now replaced by this architecturally designed undercover imposter. Whatever your opinion, the place continues to make mouths water. It is home to Rome's first vegan market stall (offering everything from animal-free edibles to cosmetics), and vendors selling handbags, clothes, shoes and homewares, but it's the food section that really shines. Lust over organic fruit and vegetables, pungent cheeses, salty salumi (cured meats), olives and seafood. There's a good choice of ready-to-cook items, from handmade pasta to polpette di spinaci (spinach dumplings) and involtini di guanciale (cured pig-cheek rolls), as well as high-quality street food. Best of the lot is Sergio Esposito's **Mordi e Vai** stall, famous for simple, scrumptious panini, freshly stuffed with combos like pork sausage and broccoli purée, vitello al ragù bianco (veal cooked with wine, pancetta and onion) and scottona (tender beef). In true Roman style, the market lies over clearly visible 1st- and 2nd-century ruins.

TAVERNA VOLPETTI

Via Alessandro Volta 8
06 574 4306
www.tavernavolpetti.it
Open Sun–Mon 11am–4pm,
Tues–Sat 11am–11pm

Taverna Volpetti is the 2.0 version of a traditional Testaccio eatery: vintage-meets-contemporary interior, clued-up yet friendly service, smart clientele and sophisticated takes on simple Italian comfort food. Spectacular cacio e pepe (pasta with pecorino romano cheese and black pepper) shares the page with less ubiquitous gnocchi con fonduta d'alpeggio (gnocchi in a cheese fondue) and fettucine con salsiccia e spuntature (fettucine with pork sausage and spare ribs). Revamped desserts can include a show-stopping deconstructed bavarese di ricotta with chestnuts cooked in vincotto (a sweet syrup made from unfermented grape must) and the layered pastry millefoglie filled with passionfruit Chantilly cream is a favourite. Much of the produce is bought fresh from Testaccio's famous market, while the selection of salumi (cured meats) and 150-plus cheeses includes some deliciously rare options. Well-versed staff oversee a cellar of more than 230 mostly Italian wines. Book ahead for Friday and Saturday dinner or Sunday lunch.

3.

4.

4.

3.

3.

4.

5.

FELICE A TESTACCIO

Via Mastro Giorgio 29
06 574 6800
http://feliceatestaccio.it
Open Mon–Sun 12.30–3pm &
7–11.30pm

You'll need to book at least a week ahead to score a table at this popular, linen-lined old-timer. Lunch and dinner are divided into sittings, and the drawcard is stubbornly traditional Roman cuisine, faithful right down to the rotating daily specials. The menu launches straight into hearty primi (first courses) such as tonnarelli cacio e pepe (spaghetti-like pasta with pecorino romano cheese and cracked pepper), mixed directly at your table. Even better, in my opinion, is the ravioli alla Felice, a wonderfully fresh, herbaceous filled pasta of salted ricotta, cherry tomatoes, basil, mint, oregano, thyme and marjoram. From trippa (tripe) to lingua di manzo (beef tongue) and pajata (unweaned calf intestines), Testaccio's old obsession with offal is evident in the choice of secondi (mains), with less daring options including comforting polpette al sugo (meatballs in a tomato sauce). If it's on offer, end on a high note with the cherry and ricotta crostata (tart).

ROMEO CHEF & BAKER

Piazza dell'Emporio 28
06 3211 0120
https://romeo.roma.it
Open Tues–Sat 4pm–2am, Sun
12pm–2am

Burrowing in at the base of Aventine Hill, this behemoth gourmet deli, bar and restaurant is the love child of Michelin-starred chef Cristina Bowerman and restaurateur Fabio Spada. The deli section is a what's what of niche edibles, from 60-month-aged Parmigiano-Reggiano to rare spalla cruda (cured pork shoulder). Cristina's Puglian origins show in delicacies like scaldatelli (boiled taralli biscuits) and jars of cime di rapa battuto alla contadina, an earthy spread made with eggplant, zucchini, tomatoes, onions, capers, apple vinegar and herbs. Romeo also does freshly baked loaves and pizza al taglio (pizza by the slice), and even sells handy 'cooking kits' with pre-prepared ingredients for time-poor cooks. While reviews of the rear contemporary Italian restaurant are mixed, there's no faulting its centrepiece bar. Perch yourself on a stool, order a well-crafted cocktail and nibble on speciality salumi (cured meats), cheeses or – my favourite – a combo of fresh buffalo mozzarella and salty anchovy fillets.

7.

PECORINO

Via Galvani 64
06 5725 0539
www.ristorantepecorino.it
Open Tues–Sun 12.30–3pm &
7.30–11.30pm

It's only apt that this family-run stalwart shares its name with a piquant cheese. After all, it's a main ingredient in fettuccine alla gricia, Pecorino's legendary pasta dish. The version here is generous and decadent, with the salty, juicy kick of guanciale (cured pig's cheek) punctuating a creamy, tangy pecorino cheese sauce. While the secondi (mains) include a trio of seafood dishes, the emphasis is squarely on meaty Roman classics, among them involtini alla romana (veal with prosciutto and sage), coda alla vaccinara (oxtail stew) and – for the more adventurous – trippa alla romana (tripe in a tomato sauce). If you haven't combusted yet, leave room for the exceptional tiramisu, the unapologetic richness of which is skilfully balanced by its not-too-sweet coffee-soaked sponge. Food aside, one of the things I love most about this place is the atmosphere: its mix of old photographs, Rome-themed artworks and strung chillies draws everyone from elegant middle-aged couples to the odd tee-clad millennial.

8.

TRAPIZZINO

Via Giovanni Branca 88
06 4341 9624
www.trapizzino.it
Open Tues–Sun 12pm–1am

Pizzaiolo (pizza maker) Stefano Callegari is the brains behind the trapizzino, a hybrid street food that has become a local cult hit. It's a fusion of the popular triangular tramezzino sandwich and slowly leavened pizza dough into a focaccia-like creation. Soft and spongy with a crisp crust, trapizzini can be filled with your choice of classic Roman flavours. Scan the counter for pots filled with made-from-scratch parmigiana di melanzane (eggplant parmigiana), coda alla vaccinara (oxtail stew), or lingua in salsa verde (tongue in a salsa verde). Herbivores won't go hungry either, with flesh-free fillings including anything from carciofi alla romana (Roman-style artichokes) to broccoli mandorle e pecorino (broccoli with almonds and pecorino cheese) and vegetable caponata. One or two should appease most appetites, and at circa €4 a pop, this is one of the cheapest feeds in town. Other handy branches in central Rome include the Mercato Centrale food hall inside Termini train station.

7.

8.

Testaccio's southern end is flanked by the tranquil, verdant **Cimitero Acattolico di Roma** (Via Caio Cestio 5). The city's 'Protestant' cemetery is the resting place of famous residents including English Romantic poets John Keats and Percy Bysshe Shelley, as well as Welsh Neoclassical sculptor John Gibson. Seek out the *Angel of Grief*, a deeply moving sculpture created by American artist William Wetmore Story for the grave of his wife, Emelyn Story.

A short walk north lies Via Galvani, which flanks the back of the Nuovo Mercato di Testaccio (see p. 128). Facing the site is a 30-metre-high **mural** of a wolf bracing for attack. This striking piece is by Belgian street artist ROA, who completed it in one short day.

A few blocks to the east is the neighbourhood's main thoroughfare of Via Marmorata, which divides the neighbourhood from Aventine Hill, one of Rome's original seven hills. From here, Via Asinio Pollione (which becomes Via di Porta Lavernale) leads up to the **Villa del Priorato di Malta** (Piazza dei Cavalieri di Malta), the Roman headquarters of the Sovereign Order of Malta (Knights of Malta). You won't be able to enter, but peer through its famous green-door keyhole for a novel view of St Peter's Basilica's imposing dome (see p. 122), the work of Renaissance over-achiever Michelangelo.

Next door is the early Christian **Basilica di Santa Sabina** (Piazza Pietro d'Illiria 1), which dates back to the 5th century. While the carved cypress doors are original, the basilica's beautiful cloister is a 13th-century addition.

Francesca Metta and Agnese Consorsi are the owners of 86.HaloStreet, a boutique selling unique garments made entirely by hand in the heart of Testaccio.

Tram Depot (*see* p. 126) occupies a green corner on Via Marmorata. It's like a petite urban oasis and a great place if you're looking for a quiet retreat for a coffee or aperitif to enjoy under the trees.

Trapizzino (*see* p. 132) serves simple yet irresistible triangles of pizza bianca stuffed with traditional Roman specialities. It's the perfect union between innovation and tradition, and while it's now famous across the world, it was born right here in Testaccio.

Nuovo Mercato di Testaccio (*see* p. 128) is popular with those who love to source fresh produce on a daily basis, but you'll also find stalls selling innovative, design-conscious products. We especially love the street food here, which ranges from traditional bites to offerings from lauded chefs.

L'oasi della Birra (Piazza Testaccio 41) is a fabulous beer bar and eatery, with an excellent selection of brews and wines, and a generous aperitivo buffet in the evenings. When it's warm, sip your drink on Piazza Testaccio, the true heart of the neighbourhood.

A skeletal gasometer, graffiti-strewn factory buildings and loft-like eateries and bars speak to Rome's edgier side in traditionally working-class Ostiense. Dramatic conversions punctuate the district, among them an aircraft terminal turned Italian food emporium and a power plant turned ancient-art museum. Street-art fans Snapchat the super-sized murals on Via del Porto Fluviale, while those spiritually inclined worship at Basilica di San Paolo Fuori le Mura (see p. 147), built over St Paul's burial site.

East of the Line B metro tracks lies peculiar Garbatella, an early 20th-century garden suburb sporting some of the capital's unique domestic architecture.

Map labels:
- VIA ANTONIO PACINOTTI
- PONTE DELL'INDUSTRIA
- Fiume Tevere (River Tiber)
- LUNGOTEVERE
- RIVA OSTIENSE
- VIA LUIGI PIERANTONI
- VITTORIO GASSMAN
- Gasometro
- Teatro India
- VIA TIRONE

24   JUN 8876

SHOP AND EAT
1 EATALY

EAT
2 TRATTORIA PENNESTRI
3 DAR MOSCHINO
4 ALTROVE
5 LE MAISONNETTE RISTROT
6 GELATERIA LA ROMANA

EAT AND DRINK
7 RISTORANTE ANGELINA AL PORTO FLUVIALE

OSTIENSE AND GARBATELLA

TRATTORIA
PENNESTRI

VIA DELLA
STAZIONE OSTIENSE

ROMA
OSTIENSE

TECHNICOLOR
ALIEN MURAL

RISTORANTE ANGELINA
AL PORTO FLUVIALE

Abitart
Hotel

VIA DEL PORTO FLUVIALE

VIA PELLEGRINO MATTEUCCI

GELATERIA
LA ROMANA

PIZZERIA
OSTIENSE

VIA DEL COMMERCIO

VIA GIACOMO BOVE

VIA FEDERICO NANSEN

BENZONI

EATALY

ALTROVE

PIAZZALE 12 OTTOBRE 1492

VIA FRANCESCO
ANTONIO PIGAFETTA

FRANCESCO

NEGRI

VIA GIROLAMO

VIA ANTON
DA NOLI

VIA
DELLA
MOLETTA

OSTIENSE

VIA

OSTIENSE
QUARTIERE X

MUNICIPIO
VIII

VIA PROSPERO ALPINO

CIRCONVALLAZIONE

MUSEI
CAPITOLINI
CENTRALE
MONTEMARTINI

PONTE
SETTIMIA
SPIZZICHINO

OSTIENSE

LE
MAISONNETTE
RISTROT

VIA NICOLO DA PISTOIA

CAFFARO

ALEXIS
MURAL

GARBATELLA

0   100 m

VIA DEGLI
ARGONAUTI

VIA GIUSEPPE LIBETTA

OSTIENSE

N

VIA DAVID SAULIERI

VIA GIACINTO PULLINO

Parco dei
Caduti
del Mare

VIA GIOVANNI
ANDREA BADOERO

VIA

VIA DOMENICO
MUNARI

Piazza
Giancarlo
Vallauri

Piazza
Pantero
Pantera

Largo
Giovanni
Ansaldo

CIALDI

VIA DELLA GARBATELLA

VIA LUIGI FINCATI

VIA OBIZZO
GUIDOTTI

ALESSANDRO

VIA ALBERTO GUGLIELMOTTI

DAR
MOSCHINO

Piazza
Bartolomeo
Romano

TEATRO
PALLADIUM

VIA GIULIO ROCCO

Parco
Marcella e
Maurizio
Ferrara

LUIGI ORLANDO

VIA

1.

EATALY

Piazzale XII Ottobre 1492
06 9027 9201
www.eataly.net
Open Mon–Sun 9am–12am

The world's largest Eataly store is a Disneyland for food lovers. Its four sprawling floors are divided into a series of shopping and dining areas dedicated to Italian gastronomy. You'll find stands selling in-season fruit and vegetables, regional cheeses and salumi (cured meats), fiery chillies, meats and glistening seafood, not to mention anything and everything from artisanal pasta and chocolate-coated grissini to wines, liqueurs and Italian-made kitchenware. You'll even find a culinary-themed book section, with a handful of titles in English. The mark-up tends to be higher than standard supermarkets, but it's the best place for scoring harder-to-find pantry treats. If you're feeling peckish, sit-down dining options include panini, burgers, pasta and wood-fired pizza, fresh seafood and meat dishes. Given its size and high turnover, it's especially handy on a Friday or Saturday night if you haven't made a reservation anywhere for dinner. For sweets, try waist-expanding gelato, creamy pastries and super-cute marzipan sweets fashioned like mini loquats and prickly pears.

LOCAL TIP

For the classic Roman pizza experience, tuck into charred thin-crust slices at evenings-only Pizzeria Ostiense (Via Ostiense 56).

TRATTORIA PENNESTRI

Via Giovanni da Empoli 5
06 574 2418
Open Tues–Thurs 7–11pm,
Fri–Sun 12–3pm & 7–11pm

Shared ideas about good food, wine and hospitality led Danish-Italian chef Tommaso Pennestri and Argentinian-born sommelier Valeria Payero to open Trattoria Pennestri,a thoughtful, modern take on the classic Italian trattoria and its culinary traditions. Childhood memories and creative impulses conspire in seasonal creations like pasta e fagioli (pasta with beans), freshened with the addition of cicoria (chicory) and peperoncino affumicato (smoked chilli), or heartening saltimbocca di polpette e patata schiacciata al limone (meatballs wrapped in buttery prosciutto and served with lemon-scented potato mash and crispy sage). An emphasis on premium produce extends to the fish, caught wild in Italian waters. For an unforgettable finale, order the chocolate mousse with salt flakes and rosemary. Wines are Valeria's passion, and her ever-changing offerings include a number of biodynamic options from smaller producers. The wall mural depicts the chef's father, uncle, grandparents and family dog. Book ahead, especially if dining later in the week.

3.

DAR MOSCHINO

Piazza Benedetto Brin 5
06 513 9473
Open Mon–Sat 12.45–2.30pm
& 7.45–10.30pm

Gen X Romans suffer
pangs of nostalgia at this
barrel-vaulted, pine-clad
'70s-style trattoria. Set in
one of Garbatella's eccentric,
medieval-inspired villas, it
dishes up a hit-list of old-
school comforters, from
pasta con fagioli (pasta with
beans) and trippa (tripe), to
a notable polpette al sugo
(meatballs in tomato sauce).
If you're a carnivore, do
not miss the rigatoni alla
gricia, a classic Roman pasta
dish made with guanciale
(cured pig's cheek) and
pecorino cheese – it's hands
down one of my favourite
renditions in the city. There
is a written menu, but trust
the waiters, who'll happily
confirm what's looking
especially good on the day.
If you're lucky, it might be
fresh seppie (cuttlefish), best
served as seppie con piselli
(cuttlefish with peas and
tomato sauce), good enough
for the most fastidious Roman
nonna (grandmother). Wine
offerings are less impressive,
but this simply adds to Dar
Moschino's authenticity.
As to the plethora of horse-
themed art on the walls,
the owner is a fan of all
things equine.

4.

ALTROVE

Via Girolamo Benzoni 34
06 574 6576
www.altroveristorante.it
Open Mon–Tues 12.15–4pm
& 6–8.30pm, Wed–Fri
12.15–4pm & 6pm–12am,
Sat 8am–4pm & 6pm–12am,
Sun 9am–4pm (closed Sun
mid-June–Sept)

Look closely at the counters
and you'll notice upcycled
fragments of vintage doors,
sourced from old cantinas
in Umbria. While they make
for quirky design detail, they
also reflect Altrove's motto:
Porte aperte sul mondo
(Doors open on the world).
A social enterprise run by
a non-profit organisation,
this light, contemporary
cafe-bistro offers hospitality
training and employment
for Italians, the children of
immigrants and refugees.
It also serves fresh, healthy,
vibrant grub reflecting the
different cultures of its staff,
such as Peruvian-inspired
lime-marinated ceviche
with white habanero and
mint or Tunisian-inspired
mechouia, a dish of grilled
vegetables, tuna tartare and
sugar-marinated egg yolk.
Lunch offers a cheaper,
paired back menu. Best of
all, Altrove uses ethical,
eco-friendly produce, which
means ordering something
sweet from the in-house
pasticceria is morally
virtuous… Right?

4.

4.

3.

5.

LE MAISONNETTE RISTROT

Via Giacinto Pullino 103
06 8376 5543
http://ristrot.it
Open Mon–Sun 11am–2am

If you're pining for the countryside, make believe at this bucolic little all-day restaurant. Wedged between the landmark Settimia Spizzichino bridge and Garbatella metro station, the restored country house comes complete with mismatched furniture, ceramic cats, a retro telephone, vintage paintings and photographs, and a leafy garden with alfresco tables. Siblings Alessandro and Susanna Sipione started the place as a passion project, and the vibe is youthful, friendly and relaxed. The menu is a seasonal affair, with thoughtfully presented dishes like polpette di baccalà (salted-cod 'meatballs'), homemade mayonnaise and pennyroyal; chicche (small potato gnocchi) with cannellini beans, baccalà and spicy 'nduja (spreadable Calabrian salami); or perhaps roasted mackerel paired with smoked scamorza cheese, goose mortadella and eggplant mince. These may sound ambitious, but fundamentally they're Italian comfort food. The wine list is interesting and heavily Italian, and there's a small selection of craft beer on tap for hops enthusiasts.

LOCAL TIP
Garbatella's Nero Vaniglia (Circonvallazione Ostiense 201) peddles delectable tortine monoporzioni (bite-sized desserts), plus breakfast-friendly cornetti (Italian croissants) and other pastries.

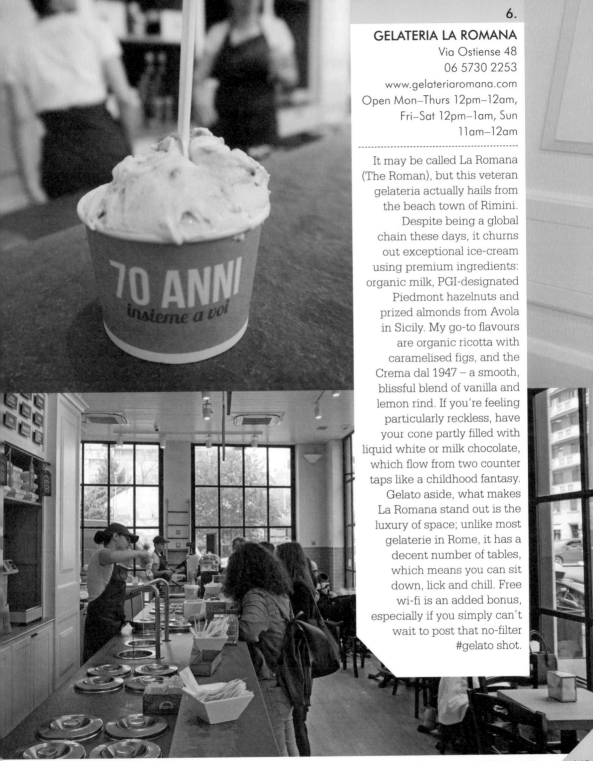

GELATERIA LA ROMANA

Via Ostiense 48
06 5730 2253
www.gelateriaromana.com
Open Mon–Thurs 12pm–12am,
Fri–Sat 12pm–1am, Sun
11am–12am

It may be called La Romana (The Roman), but this veteran gelateria actually hails from the beach town of Rimini. Despite being a global chain these days, it churns out exceptional ice-cream using premium ingredients: organic milk, PGI-designated Piedmont hazelnuts and prized almonds from Avola in Sicily. My go-to flavours are organic ricotta with caramelised figs, and the Crema dal 1947 – a smooth, blissful blend of vanilla and lemon rind. If you're feeling particularly reckless, have your cone partly filled with liquid white or milk chocolate, which flow from two counter taps like a childhood fantasy. Gelato aside, what makes La Romana stand out is the luxury of space; unlike most gelaterie in Rome, it has a decent number of tables, which means you can sit down, lick and chill. Free wi-fi is an added bonus, especially if you simply can't wait to post that no-filter #gelato shot.

7.

RISTORANTE ANGELINA AL PORTO FLUVIALE

Via del Porto Fluviale 5F
06 8971 5031
www.ristoranteangelina.com
Open Sun–Thurs 7.30am–11pm,
Fri–Sat 7.30am–11.30pm

If you're an indecisive oenophile, Angelina has your back. Aperitivo options include a good-value wine degustation (€15), comprising four tastings and a tagliere (board) of cheeses and cured meats. Wines are grouped by region, and traverse the cool hillsides of Piedmont to the sun-bleached vineyards of Sicily. The platter is laden with moreish bites, from citrus-infused coppa (cured pork shoulder or neck) and pistachio-infused mortadella (sausage), to fresh ricotta and nutty gorgonzola. Then there's the fabulous fit-out: a softly lit bistro-cum-conservatory where tasselled lampshades and velvet cushions conspire with lush palms, ferns and potted ficus trees. The venue is open all day, making it just as handy for morning cappuccinos and cakes, a lunchtime panino or dinnertime bowl of strozzapreti pasta with asparagus, guanciale (cured pig's cheek) and piquant pecorino. And while the kitchen closes before 12am, the bar usually remains open well after.

Ostiense is a hotspot for street art. Don't miss Italian artist Blu's technicolor **alien mural** on the former aeronautical barracks, located at the corner of Via del Porto Fluviale and Via delle Conce. A separate **mural** on the building's eastern side (also by Blu) offers a dystopian view of industry and 'progress'.

Further west, the neighbourhood's **fish market** (Via del Porto Fluviale 67) is an apt setting for Italian-born, Berlin-based Agostino Iacurci's playful **mural** of a goggles-and-cap-clad man swimming among fish. While you're here, don't forget to peer at the side wall, which features an intriguing **work** by Miami-born artist Axel Void. The mural depicts the back of a mysterious young woman, her white collar superimposed with a small circle in which local workers from yesteryear are depicted, frozen in time.

Further south you can find Blu's mural **Alexis** (Via Ostiense 122), a tribute to Athenian teen Alexandros Grigoropoulos, shot dead by police in 2008. The teen's murder sparked protests and riots across Greece.

Close by is the unique **Musei Capitolini Centrale Montemartini** (Via Ostiense 106); its notable collection of ancient sculpture and mosaics is dramatically juxtaposed against brooding industrial architecture. The Musei Capitolini's main branch is on Piazza del Campidoglio in central Rome. Established in 1471, it's considered the world's oldest public museum.

Via Ostiense continues south to the **Basilica di San Paolo Fuori** le Mura (Via Ostiense 190). This pious behemoth is the second largest church in Rome (after St Peter's Basilica, *see* p. 122) and the third largest church in the world, erected on the site where St Paul was buried after his martyrdom in 67 CE. Commissioned by Emperor Constantine in the 4th century, it suffered extensive damage in a fire in 1823. Features that survived the flames include the 5th-century triumphal arch, the 12th-century Romanesque Paschal candlestick and the 13th-century Gothic tabernacle above the High Altar. The Cosmati mosaics that decorate the cloisters of the adjacent Benedictine abbey also date from the 13th century.

Just east of the Musei Capitolini Centrale Montemartini, the contemporary **Ponte Settimia**

Spizzichino reaches the Garbatella quarter, whose notable buildings include curvaceous arts centre **Teatro Palladium** (Piazza Bartolomeo Romano). It's one of several buildings in the district that was designed by prolific 20th-century architect Innocenzo Sabbatini. The streets surrounding the theatre harbour some wonderfully eclectic examples of early 20th-century domestic architecture.

TO MAP RIGHT
(ALONG
VIA PANNONIA
& VIA DELLA
NAVICELLA)

Chiesa della
Natività di
Nostro Signore
Gesù Cristo

EPIRO

Celio revels in contradiction: touts, tourist menus and gay-friendly bars sidle up against medieval churches and rambling, verdant orchards. The grid of streets closest to the Colosseum (see p. 157) are the busiest and most touristy, while those to the south are the greenest, sleepiest and most atmospheric. This is a neighbourhood of hidden secrets, from subterranean pagan ruins and early Christian frescoes, to off-the-radar shops peddling rare LPs and local design.

To the south-east lies San Giovanni, an area which, despite its glorious basilica (see p. 157), prefers a comfortably domestic life of neighbourly bars, grocery vendors and the odd in-the-know dining hotspot.

24   JUN 8ST6

SHOP
1 Soul Food
EAT
2 Epiro
3 Mangio Bio

17

EAT AND DRINK
4 Divin Ostilia
5 Il Pentagrappolo

CELIO AND
SAN GIOVANNI

⊕ BASILICA
DI SAN PIETRO
IN VINCOLI

VIA EUDOSSIANA

VIA DELLE SETTE SALE

Parco del Colle Oppio

Parco di Traiano

VIA DELLE TERME DI TRAIANO

OPPIO

Terme di
Traiano
(ruins)

MONTE

VIA DI MECENATE

Sette
Sale
(ruins)

VIA MECENATE

VIALE DEL

Terme di
Traiano
(ruins)

VIA DEGLI ORTI

MONTI
RIONE I

Parco del Colle Oppio

VIALE SERAPIDE

VIALE DELLA DOMUS AUREA

VIALE FORTUNATO MIZZI

VIA MECENATE

VIA GIOVANNI PASCOLI

Chiesa di
San Giuseppe
di Cluny

VIA ANGELO POLIZIANO

■ Hotel
Edera

VIA RUGGERO BONGHI

VIA LUDOVICO MURATORI

Colosseum

Ludus
Magnus
(ruins)

VIA

🚻

⊞ 🚹🚺 **COMING OUT**

⊕

**COLOSSEO/
SALVI N.**

LABICANA

LABICANA

🚇

VIA LABICANA

● **DIVIN
OSTILIA**

VIA DI SAN

VIA DEI

VIA OSTILIA

SANTI

GIOVANNI

✉

BASILICA
DI SAN
CLEMENTE

IN

VIA CAPO

QUATTRO

LATERANO

VIA

D'AFRICA

CELIMONTANA

● **MANGIO
BIO** ●

VIA DEI SANTI

QUATTRO

**SOUL
FOOD**

VIA MARCO AURELIO

Hotel Capo
d'Africa

Monastero
Santi
Quattro
Coronati

Parco
del
Celio

VIA

VIA

● **IL PENTAGRAPPOLO**

VIA

VIA DEI QUERCETI

↑N

VIA

ANNIA

■ Fontana
Celimontana

0   100 m

VIA CLAUDIA

*Piazza
Celimontana*

CELIO
RIONE XIX

ROTONDO

STEFANO

MUNICIPIO I

Acquedotto
Claudio

■

SANTO

Arco di
Dolabella

🚹🚺 ■

Cappella
Policlinico
Militare

VIA DI

MONTI
RIONE I

*Villa
Celimontana*

Chiesa di
Santa Maria in
Dominica
alla Navicella

VIA DELLA NAVICELLA

**CHIESA DI
SANTO STEFANO
ROTONDO**

⊕

TO EPIRO
(SEE MAP LEFT) ↓

SOUL FOOD

Via di San Giovanni in
Laterano 194
06 7045 2025
www.haterecords.com
Open Tues–Sat 10.30am–
1.30pm & 3.30–7.30pm

Run by a seasoned music
journalist and a '90s punk-
rocker, this orange-and-blue
bolthole is a local institution,
and where serious music
nuts head to bulk up their
vinyl collections. The place
has a soft spot for music-
industry underdogs, making
its catalogue of indie-label
records especially impressive.
There's no shortage of
originals and rare treasures
covering punk, garage, new
wave, rockabilly, funk, soul,
exotica, psych, folk and
power pop. You'll even find
a small section dedicated to
Australian and New Zealand
artists. If you're into 45s,
there are around 50 crates
to browse (most are tucked
away behind the counter
so ask to see them). Music
aside, Soul Food is also
worth a pit stop for its cache
of tees, printed locally or in
the US and featuring offbeat
graphics and logos sourced
from pulp fiction and B-grade
movies. Last but not least, the
limited-edition posters are
perfect for walls in need of a
little X-factor.

2.

EPIRO

Piazza Epiro 26
06 6931 7603
Open Tues–Fri 7.30–11pm,
Sat–Sun 1–3pm & 7.30–11pm

Four young, talented friends are the force behind rising star Epiro. Chefs Marco Mattana and Marco Baldi shake up local traditions by combining creative verve, technical prowess and global influences. The result? Attention-piquing dishes that can see pillow-soft beef served with miso, marinated endive and sea-urchin mayonnaise, or perfectly cooked quail paired with prawns and a delicate ramen broth. Combining meat and fish is one of the kitchen's trademarks, alongside a signature ravioli stuffed with butter and parmesan, served with beef tartare. Opt for the good-value degustation menu for a satisfying overview. Epiro uses organic veggies from its own plot; the intriguing wine list champions small, mainly Italian and French winemakers; and the beers are all fermented with wild yeasts. Two intimate dining rooms are decorated with books, bottles, artwork and curious ceiling lights decked with plants, and there's a back patio for alfresco noshing in warmer months. Reserve a few days ahead.

3.

MANGIO BIO

Via dei Querceti 3
331 7497017
Open Mon–Fri 9am–8pm, Sat 10.30am–6.30pm

This upbeat corner health-food store draws an overwhelmingly local crowd craving something other than pizza, pasta and panini. Owners Danilo Di Giovenale and Letizia Genna greet their endless stream of regulars with hugs and easy banter, while newcomers are quickly made to feel welcome. The day's offerings are lined up at the glass counter, from which you can create a varied lunch plate. Everything is seasonal and organic, much of it cooked by Letizia herself. Depending on the time of year, options may include a warming vellutata (cream of vegetable soup), panzarotti (large calzone) filled with quinoa, spinach and ricotta, vegetable muffins, or polpette (patties) made with chickpeas, spinach and Parmigiano cheese. I love the simple, fresh vegetable dishes like broccoli with crumbed hazelnuts – a respite from traditionally rich Roman cuisine. The store stocks a variety of organic take-home products, including olive oils and marmalades; Letizia and Danilo know several of the producers, so there's often an anecdote attached.

2.

3.

2.

2.

3.

3.

4.

DIVIN OSTILIA
Via Ostilia 4
06 7049 6526
Open Mon–Sun 12pm–1am

This pocket-sized enoteca (wine bar) feels reassuringly authentic, despite its proximity to the touristy Colosseum area. It's wonderfully snug, with a wooden L-shaped bar, a handful of tables, and bottle-lined shelves. Blackboards list the day's rossi (reds) and bianchi (whites) by the glass, and the choice of bollicine (sparkling wines). Italian wines dominate, and you'll always stumble across an interesting varietal or less familiar style, such as arneis, Garda Classico or sagrantino. If you're undecided (or utterly confused), owner Stefano Anastasia and his team have a knack for steering you towards the perfect drop. The food menu includes graze-friendly snacks like oysters, cheeses, salumi (cured meats) and bruschetta, as well as pizzas, salads, warming pasta dishes and meat and fish mains. If it's on offer, tuck into the tonnarelli cacio pepe e tartufo nero (spaghetti-like pasta with pecorino romano, black pepper and flakes of black truffle). No-reservations; head in early for lunch or dinner to avoid a long wait.

LOCAL TIP
In the shadow of the Colosseum, popular, long-running gay bar Coming Out (Via di San Giovanni in Laterano 8) pumps with an international crowd in the evenings.

IL PENTAGRAPPOLO
Via Celimontana 21B
06 709 63 01
www.ilpentagrappolo.com
Open Mon–Fri 12–3pm &
6–10pm, Sat–Sun 6–10pm

A worthy haunt in Celio's sea of tourist traps, barrel-vaulted Il Pentagrappolo pours well-chosen vino. The wine list is predominantly Italian, many of the options natural and from small producers, with a number of French drops and a trickle of wines from further afield, including Lebanon. Check the blackboard for the day's offerings by the glass, which usually include a lesser-known varietal or two. Prices are reasonable, with wines by the glass around €6 and bottles from €18. Grazing options include interesting cheese and charcuterie options, such as cecina di León (cured beef hind leg from north-western Spain) or blu di Lanzo, an intense blue cheese from Italy's Piedmont region. The short lunch menu includes a good-value €12 deal, comprising a first and second course, side dish, a small sweet and water. But best are Friday and Saturday nights, when the more substantial dinner menu comes with a free serve of live jazz or blues (usually from around 9.30pm; reserve ahead).

Rome's official cathedral, the **Basilica di San Giovanni in Laterano** (Piazza di San Giovanni in Laterano 4) is an extraordinary creation. Commissioned by Constantine and consecrated in the 4th century, this was the epicentre of Christendom for a thousand years. The 18th-century facade – decorated with colossal statues of Christ, St John the Baptist, John the Evangelist and the 12 Apostles – is the work of architect and mathematician Alessandro Galilei, a relative of star-gazing Galileo. Much older than the façade are the central bronze doors, which graced the Roman Forum's Curia (Senate House) in ancient times. While Baroque architect Francesco Borromini revamped much of the interior in the 17th century, its older features include 15th-century mosaic floors and fragments of 4th-century mosaics in the apse. The basilica's cloister dates from the 13th century.

Across the street, the **Scala Santa** (Piazza di San Giovanni in Laterano 14) is climbed by pilgrims on their knees. Transported to Rome in the 4th century, these stairs are said to be the very ones that Jesus climbed to speak with Pontius Pilate in Jerusalem. Today, they lead up to the **Sancta Sanctorum**, once the Pope's private chapel.

From Piazza San Giovanni in Laterano, Via Santo Stefano Rotondo leads west to the unusual **Chiesa di Santo Stefano Rotondo** (Via di Santo Stefano Rotondo 7), famed for its gruesome 16th-century frescoes depicting the torture of early Christian martyrs. Further west, below the Basilica dei SS Giovanni e Paolo al Celio lie the Case Romane (Clivo di Scauro), vividly frescoed Roman abodes used for secretive Christian worship in the religion's early days.

Subterfuge makes way for grandeur at the nearby **Palatino** (Via San Gregorio 30), an evocative sprawl of ruins that once housed Ancient Roman rulers. According to legend, it was right here on Palatine Hill that Romulus, who was raised by a wolf, founded Rome in 753 BCE. Highlights include the 16th-century **Orti Farnesiani**, one of Europe's first botanical gardens. Demanding attention at the northeastern foot of Palatine Hill is the mighty **Colosseum** (Piazza del Colosseo), impressing the masses since 70 CE. A combination ticket is available for the Palatino, Colosseum, and adjoining **Roman Forum** (Largo della Salara Vecchia,

Piazza di Santa Maria Nova), the latter Ancient Rome's civic and political heart.

From Piazza del Colosseo, Via di San Giovanni in Laterano leads to the 12th-century **Basilica di San Clemente** (Piazza San Clemente), which sits atop a 4th-century church, itself above a 2nd-century pagan temple and 1st-century Roman abode. The basilica is worth a visit for its spectacular 12th-century mosaics and 15th-century frescoes by celebrated painter Masolino da Panicale.

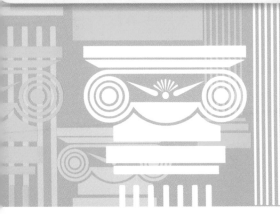

Prosperous Parioli is the holy grail of real estate, its villas and apartments home to polished professionals and pampered pooches. Foreign flags fly from embassies; fur cascades from shoulders; and tree-lined streets are awash with double-parked German imports.

The neighbourhood is predominately residential, its handful of elegant restaurants, wine bars and delis drawing lunching ladies and dashing gents partial to a little Franciacorta (sparkling wine) and Sardinian bottarga (cured fish roe). Dress up and rub shoulders; choose your dream home on Via Giuseppe Mangili; then join both rich and mortal in the sweeping parks that bookend the district.

24   JUN 8076

SHOP, EAT AND DRINK
1 Ercoli 1928
2 Enoteca Bulzoni

EAT
3 Metamorfosi
4 Spazio Niko Romito

17

EAT AND DRINK
5 Il Cigno
6 La Salsamenteria di Roberto Mangione

PARIOLI

Villa Glori

ERCOLI 1928

Chiesa di
San Luigi
Gonzaga

Piazza
Digione

**GELATERIA
DUSE**

VIA EUGENIO
VAJNA

VIA DI VILLA EMILIANI

VIA DI VILLA ELEONORA DUSE

VIA TOMMASO SALVINI

Basilica del
Sacro Cuore
Immacolato
di Maria

⊕ EUCLIDE

0   100 m

N

VIALE PARIOLI

VIA BARNABA ORIANI

VIA RUGGERO FAURO

VIA UMBERTO BOCCIONI

Hotel
Degli
Aranci

Teatro
Parioli

VIA DI VILLA SAN FILIPPO

**PARIOLI
QUARTIERE II**

VIA GUALTIERO CASTELLINI

NINO OXILIA

**VILLA
ADA**

ROMANIA

VIA FRANCESCO DENZA

VIA GIOVANNI ANTONIO MICHELI

VIA FILIPPO CIVININI

VIA PIETRO ANTONIO MICHELI

✉ **METAMORFOSI**

VIALE PARIOLI

VIA NICOLO TARTAGLIA

VIA ANTONIO ANTONELLI

**ENOTECA
BULZONI**

⊚ **IL CIGNO**

VIALE PARIOLI

Chiesa di
San Roberto
Bellarmino

**TO LA SALSAMENTERIA
DI ROBERTO
MANGIONE
(SEE MAP LEFT)**

VIA PIETRO TACCHINI

BERTOLONI

VIALE BRUNO BUOZZI

⊕ **NARDI
DAY SPA**

VIA DI VILLA SACCHETTI

MUNICIPIO II

ROSSINI
Ⓜ

**LIEGI/
UNGHERIA**
Ⓜ

**SPAZIO
NIKO
ROMITO**

VIA GIUSEPPE MANGILI

VIA MICHELE MERCATI

**PINCIANO
QUARTIERE III**

BIOPARCO
Ⓜ

VIA GIACOMO CARISSIMI

VIA SAVERIO MERCADANTE

VIA GIOVANNI PAISIELLO

Aldrovandi
Villa Borghese

ULISSE

Museo Civico
di Zoologia

ALDROVANDI

ZOOLOGICO

Parco dei
Principi
Grand Hotel
& Spa

Ⓜ **ALDROVANDI**

**GALLERIA
NAZIONALE
D'ARTE
MODERNA**

BIOPARCO DI ROMA
(zoo)

VIALE DEL GIARDINO ZOOLOGICO

VIALE DELL'UCCELLIERA

VIALE DEI DAINI

VIA PIETRO RAIMONDI

Piazzale
dei Daini

Ⓜ **GALLERIA
ARTE
MODERNA**

**TEMPIO DI
ESCULAPIO** ⊕

VILLA BORGHESE

Platani
Orientali
del Seicento

Museo
Pietro Canonica
a Villa Borghese

Parco dei
Daini

Piazzale
Scipione
Borghese

Silvano Toti
Globe
Theatre

Piazza
di Siena

**MUSEO E GALLERIA
BORGHESE** ⊕

1.

ERCOLI 1928
Viale Parioli 184
06 808 0084
http://ercoli1928.com
Open Sun–Thurs 9am–1am,
Fri–Sat 9am–2am

Ever-sleek Ercoli 1928 is a gourmet trifecta: provedore, eatery and Vermouth bar in one. The deli is a cornucopia of all things artisanal, including handcrafted balsamic vinegar from Modena's La Secchia Antica Acetaia. The cheese selection in particular is gut-busting bliss: smoked mozzarella from Battipaglia's La Fattoria Zizzona, Roccaverano goat's cheese from Piedmont's Cascina Aris, and look out for formaggio ubriaco (drunken cheese), which is bathed in wine along with skins, seeds and other sediments from the winemaking process. Otherwise, you can also happily blow the budget on speciality cured meats, sausages, smoked fish and caviar, niche mustards and mostarda (candied fruit in a mustard-oil sauce), pickled vegetables, sauces and both local and imported wines. The deli's prized goods feature on the restaurant menu as cheese and cured-meat taglieri (boards), caviar, and in more substantial dishes from linguine with anchovy essence, olives and confit tomatoes, to seasonal soups, Piedmont-style boiled meats or roast octopus.

ENOTECA BULZONI

Viale Parioli 34
06 807 0494
www.enotecabulzoni.it
Open Mon–Sat 10am–12am,
Sun 10am–7pm

Evoking a library with its shelves, ladders and balconies, Bulzoni has been peddling wine since 1929, when founder Emidio Bulzoni launched his vini e olii (a traditional shop selling wine, oil and vinegar in bulk). Emidio's son, Sergio, introduced bottled wine to the shelves mid-century, and his grandsons, Alessandro and Riccardo, have since added organic and biodynamic wine to what is now a wine shop and bar. At smart, striped banquettes, join Parioli locals over a mainly Italian wine list divided into 'Modern', 'Classic' and 'Extreme' – the latter a showcase for funky, low-interventionist or avant-garde drops. Food options are a mainly classic Roman affair (anything from pasta alla carbonara to tripe) and while generally enjoyable, they're not exceptional, so consider matching your wine with the graze-friendly prosciutti and formaggi (cheeses) that grace the marble counter. If you love olive oil, grab a bottle of Bulzoni's own, a zesty, peppery, organic oil made with olives from the family's own groves.

3.

METAMORFOSI

Via Giovanni Antonelli 30
06 807 6839
www.metamorfosiroma.it
Open Mon–Fri 12.30–2.30pm
& 8–10.30pm, Sat 8–10.30pm

Metamorfosi (Metamorphosis) seems an appropriate name for Roy Caceres' Michelin-starred restaurant. After all, the Columbian expat has transformed himself from basketball player to one of Rome's most celebrated chefs. Caceres' dishes are technically brilliant yet playful, whether it be shard-leaf tacos with soy-marinated tuna tartare, chickpea cream and lemon-drop gel; or a deconstructed carbonara, which delivers an egg cooked at 65°C and topped with parmesan foam, crispy pasta and fried pork rind. Sweet epilogues might include a popsicle that pairs white chocolate and blue cheese to spectacular effect. To properly experience Caceres' prowess, opt for the six- or 10-course degustation menu. My fondness for Metamorfosi extends to the restaurant's design: subdued lighting and a limited number of roomy tables bestow a private dinner-party vibe. The wine list is thrilling, and the waitstaff bring genuine hospitality and enthusiasm. Reserve a week or two ahead for Friday or Saturday evenings.

4.

SPAZIO NIKO ROMITO
Piazza Giuseppe Verdi 9E
06 8535 2523
www.spazionikoromito.com
Open Mon–Sun 7am–11pm

If you fancy a few pointers on Parioli style (and you should), head to this hotspot cafe-bakery. Polished waitstaff greet a constant stream of dashing regulars, and the fit-out is appropriately on trend: muted industrial greys, brass and timber. Scan the glass counters for impeccable baked treats, from must-try brioche filled with lemon cream to panforte-style pane antico loaded with dry fruits, to savoury brioche filled with tuna and artichoke. Breads are made using a combination of heirloom saragolla and solina grains from the Abruzzo region, or Type 00 flour mixed with potato. If it's breakfast time, order a serve of the pane e marmellata (bread and marmalade) – simple but delicious. Spazio's attention to quality reflects that of prolific owner Niko Romito, a chef whose restaurant Relae claims three Michelin stars. Next door is Spazio's split-level restaurant, a leafy space with a contemporary Italian menu and some unexpected vini (wines)…perhaps a natural pinot noir from Australia.

5.

IL CIGNO

Viale Parioli 16
06 808 2348
Open Mon–Sun 7.30am–9pm

Il Cigno has been clattering coffee cups since 1949. It's a neighbourhood institution, never short of locals in for their morning espresso, lunchtime bite or Sunday tray of take-away paste (pastries). Chances are you'll be served by Dora, whose 40-odd years behind the bar have seen her watch young customers turn into adults with kids of their own. Il Cigno means 'The Swan', in reference to the ancient Greek myth of Leda and the Swan. It's the theme of the eye-popping ceramic mural behind the bar. You'll find some of Rome's best cappuccinos here, ideally paired with cornetti (croissants); try the cornetto alla mandorla (with almonds). You can even opt for one made with farina di soia (soy flour). They're all made from scratch, along with the colourful pastries, cakes, biscotti, chocolates, fruit-shaped jellies and gelato (try the Mexican chocolate flavour) that grace the glass counters. Alfresco pavement seating is available for those who like to sit, sip and stare.

6.

LA SALSAMENTERIA DI ROBERTO MANGIONE

Via dei Monti Parioli 31B/C
06 3211 1318
Open Mon & Fri 7.30am–3pm & 5–9.30pm, Tues–Thurs 7.15am–3pm & 5–9pm, Sat 7.30am–2pm & 5.30–8.30pm

----

A cross between a neighbourhood deli, wine shop and impromptu evening party, La Salsamenteria wears many hats. During the day, Parioli shoppers drop by to stock up on wagyu bresaola, Brillat-Savarin cheese and fresh eggs. Come evening, oenophiles squeeze inside for fine wine, charcuterie and camaraderie. Owner and sommelier Roberto Mangione darts between tables, pouring vintage reds, slicing cheeses, and bantering with his merry band of regulars. You'll find an impressive range of champagne on his shelves, not to mention taglieri (boards) laden with lesser-known salumi (cured meats) and formaggi (cheeses) from Italy and further afield. Roberto happily regales with anecdotes about his menu items, whether it's a glass of effervescent Egly-Ouriet, a lactose-free mortadella or a rustic South Tyrolean speck. It's always a good idea to book ahead as tables are limited and demand is high, but if you don't mind standing while imbibing, slip in and see where the evening takes you.

5.

5.

LOCAL TIP
For top-notch fresh gelato, seek out retro Gelateria Duse (Via Eleonora Duse 1B) simply known as 'Da Giovanni' to locals.

6.

Hang out with Impressionists, Futurists, Spacialists and Abstract Expressionists at the **Galleria Nazionale d'Arte Moderna** (GNAM; Viale delle Belle Arti 131), located on Parioli's western fringes. The gallery houses Italy's largest collection of 19th- and 20th-century art, with works by homegrown greats such as Antonio Canova, Umberto Boccioni and Lucio Fontana, as well as foreign heavyweights like Monet, Degas, Van Gogh, Cézanne, Rodin, Klimt and Pollock. Dating from 1911, the colonnaded building is richly ornamented and imposing, designed by noted architect Cesare Bazzani.

GNAM looks out at the northern end of **Villa Borghese**, an 80-hectare park that sprawls south to Via Vittorio Veneto and west towards Piazza del Popolo.

Step inside to wander around the nearby lake and its 18th-century **Tempio di Esculapio** (Temple of Aesculapius) framing an Ancient Roman statue of the god of medicine and healing. The statue was discovered inside the mausoleum of Augustus, first emperor of the Roman Empire.

Further downhill, Viale delle Belle Arti leads to Pope Julius III's 16th-century pad, **Villa Giulia**. The palace is now the **Museo Nazionale Etrusco** (Piazzale di Villa Giulia), and its collection of Etruscan and pre-Roman artefacts is unparalleled in Italy. These include the *Sarcofago degli Sposi* (Sarcophagus of the Betrothed), a 6th-century BCE terracotta funerary monument depicting a reclining couple; it's widely considered a masterpiece of Etruscan art. Admission also

includes entry to neighbouring **Villa Poniatowski**, its own archaeological hoard hailing from Italy's ancient Umbri and Latin peoples.

If you're at the eastern end of Parioli, luxuriate in nature at **Villa Ada** (Via Salaria), a 180-hectare sweep of lawns, woods and lakes once called home by Italy's King Vittorio Emanuele III. It's now a veritable backyard for the pariolini (Parioli locals), who head here to jog, cycle and walk their dogs. Come summer, they also head here for **Roma Incontra il Mondo**, the city's popular world-music festival.

Just east of Villa Ada lurks the ancient **Catacombe di Priscilla** (Via Salaria 430), a network of subterranean tombs and chambers dating back to between the 2nd and 5th centuries. Numerous early Christian popes and martyrs were laid to rest here and its early 3rd-century depiction of the Virgin Mary is said to be the oldest in existence. Visits to the catacombs are by guided tour only, which run roughly every 30 minutes during the day from Tuesdays to Sundays.

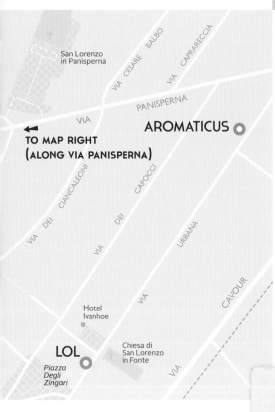

When Rome was Caput Mundi (Capital of the World), Monti was Suburra, a dense, gritty red-light district and the childhood home of Julius Caesar. While the odd sex worker still trades here discreetly, modern-day Monti is about understated cool and bohemian sensibilities. Intimate, steep, ivy-draped streets are home to one-off artisan studios, independent fashion ateliers and vintage stores, cosy eateries and, in the evenings, crowded, convivial wine bars.

The neighbourhood's communal lounge room is Piazza della Madonna dei Monti, its drinking holes and Renaissance fountain drawing night-time crowds in search of alfresco camaraderie and perhaps a little Latin flirtation.

24   JUN 8876

ƒHOP
1 Lol
2 Tina ƒondergaard
3 Nora P
4 Le Gallinelle
5 JoLeCreo
6 Mercato Monti
7 Pulp

17

EAT
8 Aromaticus
EAT AND DRINK
9 Ai Tre ƒcalini
DRINK
10 ƒacripante Gallery

MONTI

JOLECREO

TINA
SONDERGAARD

LE GALLINELLE

NORA P

SACRIPANTE
GALLERY

AI TRE
SCALINI

PULP

RADIATION
RECORDS

MUNICIPIO I

Hotel
Anfiteatro
Flavio

MONTI
RIONE I

LE NOU

Santi Sergio
e Bacco
in Suburra

Casa
Santa
Sofia

LOL

Piazza della
Madonna
dei Monti

Hotel
Duca
d'Alba

Santa
Maria
ai Monti

MERCATO
MONTI

Grand
Hotel
Palatino

VIA DEL BOSCHETTO

VIA PANISPERNA

VIA MILANO

PANISPERNA

TO
AROMATICUS
& LOL
(SEE MAP LEFT)

VIA CIMARRA

VIA CLEMENTINA

VIA DEI SERPENTI

VIA DEL BOSCHETTO

VIA SAN GIUSEPPE LABRE

VIA DEL SAMBUCO

VIA DEGLI ZINGARI

VIA BACCINA

LEONINA

N

0   50 m

1.

LOL

Via Urbana 92
06 9603 8607
http://lolroma.com
Open Mon–Sun 10am–8pm

Unequivocally one of the most interesting fashion boutiques in Rome, Lol revamps women's wardrobes with sharp edits of mostly Italian and French fashion and accessories. From silk frocks to cashmere knits, the look here is understated elegance, with a focus on prints and cognoscenti labels like Forte Forte, Majestic and Jumper. The supporting cast includes Lol's own leather bags and wallets, as well as artisan jewellery from creators such as LiL Milan and Rome's own Voodoo Jewels. There's also a small selection of footwear. The branch next door offers a more hippie-chic look, with ethnic undertones and richer colours from designers including Mademoiselle, American Vintage and Mon Ami. Those after a more conceptual look should check out the branch on nearby Piazza Madonna dei Monti, where offerings include brands like Minimal 2, Crea Concept and Liviana Conti.

TINA SONDERGAARD

Via del Boschetto 1
06 9799 0565
Open Mon–Sat 10.30am–
7.30pm

Danish expat Tina Sondergaard will bring out your inner Grace Kelly at her whimsical Monti workshop and boutique. From silk blouses and inverted pleated skirts, to fitted-bodice party dresses, her gorgeous pieces burst with bold stripes, polka dots and inimitable Mid-Century style. This is fashion for individualists, and there's no shortage of one-offs and new additions. Fabrics sometimes include out-of-the-box options like furniture textiles. Best of all, most pieces can be altered to your measurements free of charge on the same day, turning an off-the-rack piece into a bespoke treasure. The store stocks matching bags and hats, designed by fellow Dane-in-Rome Christina Herup. Clients include actor Valeria Golino, singer Carmen Console, and Italy's First Lady, yet prices are digestible, with dresses retailing for circa €150. You'll find a second, newer branch at Via del Pellegrino 83, a quick walk from Campo de' Fiori.

3.

NORA P

Via Panisperna 220
06 4547 3738
http://omniweb.altervista.org/
noraP
Open by appointment

The worldly Eleonora 'Nora' Pastore has an enviable knack for mixing old and new, a fact confirmed by her atelier. This lofty space is an ever-changing treasure trove of temptation: you might find a rare Italian tea set, upcycled-zipper jewellery, vintage wristwatches, or Mid-Century coasters. The designer also sells her own pieces, the product of collaborations with various artists, artisans and architects. Past pieces I've fawned over include striking wall mirrors, a playful table made for dining *and* ping-pong duels, as well as a 1970s Italian chair reupholstered in Mid-Century Italian silk with a Persian-themed print. You can even purchase Nora P's own collection of printed fabrics. Such talent has not gone unnoticed by the movers and shakers, with clients including fashion house Fendi and prolific film director Paolo Sorrentino. Appointments can be made by emailing nora.pastore@nora-p.com.

4.

LE GALLINELLE

Via Panisperna 60
06 488 1017
www.legallinelle.com
Open Mon–Sat 11am–8pm
(year-round), Sun 12.30–8pm
(Oct–late June)

Wilma Silvestri is one of Rome's most interesting independent designers, her stylish and playful garments a balance of creativity and comfort. This is Wilma's workshop and showroom, and you'll usually find the softly spoken talent designing or sewing at her large glass table. Researching fabrics is one of Wilma's passions; she makes regular trips to the textile towns of Prato (in Tuscany) and Como (Lombardy) in search of unique finds, including vintage silks. Fabrics are all non-synthetic, and are turned into conversation pieces such as '60s-style coats with round pockets and sheepskin linings, or dramatic silk-and-wool scarves that turn any look into a statement. Prices are approachable, with scarves between €40 and €90 and dresses between €110 and €160. Also wonderful are the wrought-iron cabinets graced with must-have vintage bags – 1970s Gucci valise, anyone? Wilma's love of vintage stems back to her days hiring out costumes for film shoots.

4. 3. 4. 3. 3. 4.

Monti   173

5.

JOLECREO
Via del Boschetto 6
349 4698770
www.jolecreo.it
Open Mon–Sat 10.30am–8pm,
Sun 4–8pm

Sustainable designer Jole
Costantino has a healthy
obsession with recycling
objects. Step into her Monti
showroom and you'll find the
likes of old buttons turned
into rings, reformed zippers,
anti-vibration pads and
even parts of old car tyres
all reconfigured into striking
sculptural necklaces. Look up
for the super-cool recycled
lampshades, also for sale.
Rerouting the destiny of old
objects has been a long-held
interest for Jole, who often
used discarded objects as
clever props when working as
a fashion photographer, stylist
and visual merchandiser.
The Calabrian native still
scours old and disused textile
warehouses in Rome, Paris
and her southern home region
for interesting, forgotten finds,
among them vintage buttons
(one of her absolute favourite
items). This spirit of reuse
even sees Jole occasionally
updating her own jewellery
creations, which customers
bring in for a refresh. The
feel-good factor extends to the
prices, with most jewellery
items costing between €20
and €35.

LOCAL TIP
Off-the-radar Sottobosco
(Via Baccina 40) stocks
a refreshing collection
of handmade design
objects and playful
contemporary jewellery.

MERCATO
MONTI
URBAN
MARKET
ROMA®

MERCATO MONTI

Via Leonina 46
www.mercatomonti.com
Open Sat–Sun 10am–8pm
(closed July–Aug)

Calling Mercato Monti a 'flea market' feels a bit like calling a degustation dinner a 'feed'. More than just another local swarm of stalls, it's a sophisticated hub for creativity and quality vintage. While DJs spin ambient tunes, Rome's hip and boho-chic browse the softly lit conference hall of the Grand Hotel Palatino, its rotating cast of vendors presenting everything from statement-making contemporary jewellery to handmade bags, hats, shoes, lamps and more. It's hard not to find your next great buy, whether it be a pair of vintage sunglasses, Deco-inspired Plexiglass earrings, or a military-camouflage coat plastered with a giant Immaculate Conception image. Not that you need to open your wallet to enjoy the place: the cool crowd and see-and-be-seen vibe make the place alone worth a visit.

7.

PULP

Via del Boschetto 140
06 485 511
Open Mon 4–8pm, Tues–Sat
10am–1pm & 4–8pm

Fancy a Moschino cocktail dress? How about a silk D&G shirt, or a dashing Trussardi tie? These are the kinds of nuggets you'll find at Pulp, one of Rome's oldest vintage fashion stockists. Owners Fabio Brunaccini and Fabrizio Polanschi are seasoned style hunters, regularly scouring historic fashion centres like Naples and Florence for prized retro wearables and accessories, from silk scarves to leather wallets. Fans include fashionistas, TV celebs and social-media influencers, all of whom scan the racks for quirky frocks, playful jumpers, leather jackets and more. While the stock focuses mainly on Italian fashion from the 1960s to the '90s, a small mix of international offerings can include names like Diane Von Furstenberg, Lanvin and Dior (I once stumbled upon a bespoke 1950s kimono). Big name Italians Armani, Fendi and Missoni are peppered with the odd niche label, including Roman classic Sorelle Fontana. The owners also design their own small selection of womenswear.

8.

AROMATICUS

Via Urbana 134
06 488 1355
www.aromaticus.it
Open Mon 11.30am–4pm,
Tues–Sun 11.30am–10pm

Green thumbs and health-conscious diners rub shoulders at Aromaticus, an urban-gardening shop and cafe. Rows of potted herbs, cute tin watering cans and aprons lead you through to the intimate cafe space, lined with two communal timber tables, shelves of salubrious cooking books and a menu of wholesome, produce-driven dishes. While options are healthy, they're also democratic: sure, you can order a vegan burger or subtly spiced tofu polpette ('meatballs'), but chances are you'll also find baccalà (salted cod) carpaccio with persimmon, almond and mint, or a tartare made using top-quality Fassone beef from Piedmont. Freshly squeezed juices with combos like pear and cucumber crank up the feel-good factor even further, while a small but savvy selection of take-home pantry treats includes biodynamic chilli sauces from Tuscan-based Peperita and jars of gourmet condiments from Sicilian food emporium Fratelli Burgio. If you don't like waiting, head in by 1pm as seating is limited.

LOCAL TIPS

For a quick bite, squeeze into Zia Rosetta (Via Urbana 54), a hip sandwich shop serving up creative gourmet panini and freshly squeezed juices.

Pop into Le NoU (Via del Boschetto 111) for next-gen Roman fashion and edgy, geometric creations.

8.

7.

8.

9.

AI TRE SCALINI

Via Panisperna 251
06 4890 7495
www.aitrescalini.org
Open Mon–Sun 12.30pm–1am

This ivy-covered wine bar is a Monti institution, its local clientele of creatives, hipsters and good-timers spilling out onto the street in a stream of merriment. Scan the tightly packed blackboard for the day's vini al calice (wines by the glass), a pan-Italian offering that spans crisp, bone-dry Sicilian whites to tangy Piedmontese reds. I love that I'll usually find a varietal I'm not familiar with or one rarely offered by the glass, which means I might end up swilling an Erbaluce di Caluso or a blockbuster Amarone. The blackboard also lists a modest but well-chosen offering of draught and bottled craft beers, as well as spot-hitting bites that range from cheeses and chilli-spiked olives, to salads and coaxing pasta dishes. Head in before the 7pm rush if you don't enjoy swilling on your feet.

10.

SACRIPANTE GALLERY
Via Panisperna 59
06 4890 3495
Open Tues–Sun 6pm–2am

There's something deeply enchanting about Sacripante. Could it be the beautiful hardware-store counter turned bar, the theatrical altarpiece turned back bar, the vintage apothecary jars, or perhaps those 1940s armchairs and sofas? Whatever the reason, the surreptitious space makes for an atmospheric place to imbibe. The pared-back concrete walls host rotating exhibitions of engaging contemporary art, from both local and foreign creatives. Fuel your artistic musings with a glass of bubbly Franciacorta, a Moscow mule (with house-made ginger beer) or the signature Sacripante, a floral, vodka-based libation spiked with Fior di Sambuco, lemon and Franciacorta. Titbit: the space is named after Carlo Maria Sacripante, the 18th-century cardinal who built the convent that once occupied the building. You'll find him staring at you in the bathroom.

WHILE YOU'RE HERE

Monti skirts a number of fascinating sights. Abutting its western edge is the **Mercati di Traiano dei Fori Imperiali** (Via IV Novembre 94), a 2nd-century civic complex once thronging with shops, eateries, administrative offices and other public spaces. Often dubbed 'the world's oldest shopping mall', the site was originally part of the **Fori Imperiali** (Imperial Forums). The latter is now found on the opposite side of Via dei Fori Imperiali, a thoroughfare commissioned by Italian dictator Benito Mussolini in the 1930s. Soaring above the Mercati di Traiano is the red-brick **Torre delle Milizie**, a hulking fortified tower dating from the 13th century.

Steps away from the northern edge of Monti is the luminous Neoclassical **Palazzo delle Esposizioni** (Via Nazionale 194), where cultural events including blockbuster art exhibitions and art-house film screenings are held. The space is also home to a fantastic bookstore and Michelin-starred rooftop restaurant.

To the south of Monti, the 5th-century **Basilica di San Pietro in Vincoli** (Piazza di San Pietro in Vincoli 4A) is worth a peek for Michelangelo's ambitious *Moses* sculpture. Chipped into life in the early 16th century, the work is the centrepiece of Michelangelo's unfinished tomb for Pope Julius II (the pope is actually buried in St Peter's Basilica – see p. 122). The basilica also houses the very shackles reputedly used on St Peter at the nearby **Carcere Mamertino** (Mamertine Prison).

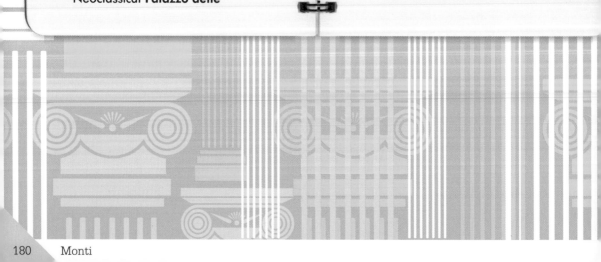

Massimiliano Rubcich is an architect, design lover and the owner of 20MQ (*see* p. 085). When he's not working, he loves exploring the streets of Monti.

Tin House (Via Leonina 30) serves high-quality Chinese dishes. Ask for the 'secret' Chinese-language menu, which offers a multitude of alternative dishes, all from the Sichuan region. The food is quite spicy.

Aromaticus (*see* p. 176) sells objects for your urban garden and serves produce from its own. Chef Luca and sommelier Francesca grow vegetables inside the shop, using them to make small, tasty, organic dishes and fresh juices.

Zia Rosetta (*see* p. 177) takes the typical Roman rosetta (rose-shaped bread roll) to another level. Order the mini sizes to sample different fillings; I love the Victoria. Perfect for a light lunch and, above all, an aperitivo.

Sacripante (*see* p. 179) is arguably the coolest drinking spot in Monti. Inspired by America's Prohibition-era speakeasies, it also hosts interesting contemporary art exhibitions.

Mercato Monti (*see* p. 175) was set up by my friend Ornella to give young designers the opportunity to showcase everything fron vintage fashion to contemporary design objects. You'll always find something inspiring.

Hasekura (Via dei Serpenti 27) is where Ito and his wife Franca serve real Japanese comfort food, as well as fresh sushi and sashimi. Book ahead.

Esquilino is Rome's tattered, multicultural welcome mat. Cult-status trattorias and pasticcerie (pastry shops) share the raffish streets with colourful South Asian grocery stores and Chinese travel agents. Accents are thick, the air heady with the scent of cumin, and the market stalls are stacked with as much bok choy as provolone.

Home to travertine-clad Termini, the city's central train station, a jumble of cheap and chintzy hotels, cookie-cutter Made-in-China shops and soulless take-aways Esquilino may be a world away from the well-heeled charm of Rome's historic heart and yet, this is one of the city's most richly textured neighbourhoods.

ESQUILINO

24   JUN 8076

SHOP
1 SiTenne
2 Millerecords
3 Roma Liuteria
4 Nuovo Mercato Esquilino

17

EAT
5 Trattoria Monti
6 Panella
7 Pasticceria Regoli
DRINK
8 Salotto Caronte

NAPOLEONE III

Giardino
dell'Acquario
Romano

Casa
dell'Architettura

Chiesa di
Sant'Antonio
Abate
all'Esquilino

Hotel
Montreal
Hotel d'Este

VIA NAPOLEONE III

VIA RATTAZZI

VIA PRINCIPE

VIA URBANO

VIA CARLO ALBERTO

VIA FILIPPO

VIA ALFREDO

CAPPELLINI

TURATI

Hotel
Filippo
Roma

VIA GIOVANNI GIOLITTI

TERMINI
LAZIALI

ESQUILINO
RIONE XV

Sant'Eusebio
all'Esquilino

AMEDEO

MAMIANI

VIA PRINCIPE

NUOVO
MERCATO
ESQUILINO

TO
ROMA LIUTERIA
(SEE MAP LEFT)

VIA PELLEGRINO ROSSI

TRATTORIA
MONTI

VIA DELLO STATUTO

Porta
Alchemica

PIAZZA
VITTORIO
EMANUELE (MA)

VITTORIO
EMANUELE

AMEDEO

PASTICCERIA
REGOLI

PANELLA

VIA

PIAZZA

Giardino Nicola Calipari

MUNICIPIO I

VIA BUONARROTI

VIA VITTORIO EMANUELE II

Hotel
Napoleon

VIA MERULANA

VIA

VIA GIUSTI

FERRUCCIO

VIA

VIA MACHIAVELLI

SALOTTO
CARONTE

PIAZZA DANTE

VIA CONTE VERDE

VIA EMANUELE

CAIROLI

Chiesa di
San Giuseppe
di Cluny

VIA ANGELO POLIZIANO

VIA

VIA CARLO BOTTA

MONTI
RIONE I

VIA GUICCIARDINI

Chiesa di
Sant'Anna
al Laterano

VIA MERULANA

MILLERECORDS

VIA

Giardino
Mary Ed
Hasib Begum

ALFIERI

VIA TASSO

SITENNE

BIXIO

FILIBERTO

0   50 m

N

GALILEI

Chiesa di
Santa Maria
Immacolata
all'Esquilino

VIA ARIOSTO

VIALE MANZONI

Hotel
Milton

MANZONI

MANZONI (MA)

VIA RUGGERO

BONGHI

183

1.

SITENNE

Via Petrarca 1
06 7725 0991
www.sitenne.com
Open Mon–Fri 10.30am–7pm,
Sat 11am–8pm

- -

More than just a vintage store, SiTenne is a grassroots hub for creativity and sustainability, repurposing vintage fashion, fabrics and accessories, and hosting occasional special events like book launches. The exceptional collection of vintage clothing means you could stumble upon a late 19th-century blouse, a 1920s cocktail dress, or a boho '80s frock with Art Deco panelling. Men's threads include dashing jackets, ties, shirts and denim, while accessories for both men and women include footwear, hats, belts and bags. Co-owner Alberta Spezzaferro's knowledge of each piece is outstanding. She's also known for her honesty: if something doesn't look great on you, she'll tell you, and help you find something better. If it's just a tweak you need, SiTenne offers a tailoring service, with most alterations ready within 24 to 48 hours. Opening times can vary; check online for updates.

LOCAL TIP
To score coveted Fausto Santini shoes for men and women, hit outlet store Giacomo Santini (Via Cavour 106).

2

MILLERECORDS
Via Merulana 91
06 7049 0109
www.millerecords.it
Open Mon 4–7.30pm, Tues–
Sat 10am–7.30pm

Millerecords has been spinning vinyl since the heady 1960s, when founder Carlo Marignoli opened the original store in Via dei Mille (hence the store's name). Finger through the stacks and you might stumble upon an album of erotic madrigals, music by English Renaissance composer John Dowland or a rare Italian release of Pink Floyd's *The Piper at the Gates of Dawn*, sans Syd Barrett on the sleeve. I've even found Italian collector editions of LPs by The Beatles. The focus is predominantly on pre-loved classical, jazz and classic rock/pop LPs, with a selection of 45RPM records, rarer 78RPMs, CDs and a small selection of cassette tapes. You'll even find back copies of Prisma, a nine-issue music magazine established by Carlo and featuring articles written by some of Italy's foremost music journalists. Also check out the prized copy of Patti Smith's *Horses*, complete with a handwritten message of appreciation from the American punk goddess herself.

3.

ROMA LIUTERIA
Via di Santa Maria Maggiore 150
339 3517677
www.romaliuteria.it
Open Mon–Sat
10am–1pm & 3–7pm

Time stands comfortingly still in Mathias Menanteau's basement workshop. The talented young artisan is one of Rome's most respected instrument makers and restorers, his quartet creations sought after by both professionals and passionate amateurs. His passion began while studying classical guitar; he crafted his own instrument, and then he followed up with his first violin. These are well-trained hands that have studied around the world, from England, Berlin, Paris and New York to Italy's own illustrious violin-making centre, the city of Cremona. The French expat crafts his instruments using spruce from the Dolomites and maple from the Balkans or southern Germany. Violins start at €3000, with both ready- and custom-made instruments available. At his rustic 19th-century work table, Mathias recalls a modern-day Geppetto, lovingly crafting instruments and tending to those old and worn. Even if you're not in the market for strings, the workshop is worth a quick peek. Appointments are appreciated.

4.

NUOVO MERCATO ESQUILINO

Via Filippo Turati 160
Open Mon & Wed–Thurs
5am–3pm, Tues & Fri–Sat
5am–5pm

To experience a side of
Rome not flaunted on
postcards, dive into the
city's most multicultural
market. Here, Italian nonne
(grandmothers) rub shoulders
with Filipino neighbours,
while Bangladeshi vendors
shout out 'ni hao' (hello)
to bargain-hunting local
Chinese cooks. It's a souk-
like atmosphere, heaving
with both Italian staples and
harder-to-find ingredients
that satisfy migrants wanting
a taste of home. Prosciutti
and olives hanging in myriad
hues and sizes share the
limelight with halal meats,
rows of technicolour spices
and grains, and a cast of fresh
fruits and vegetables ranging
from taro root and dates,
to plantains and ampalaya
(bitter melon). A second,
less intriguing, market hall
stocks clothing and textiles,
including luridly coloured
fabrics for eye-catching saris.

5.

TRATTORIA MONTI

Via di San Vito 13
06 446 6573
Open Tues–Sat 1–2.45pm &
8–10.45pm, Sun 1–2.45pm

When I simply cannot
stomach *another* carbonara,
I seek refuge in this casually
refined bastion of cucina
marchigiana (Le Marche
cuisine). Owner Franca
Marzioni has been cooking
up a storm since 1972,
guided by her mother's
example and serving up
elegant, earthy dishes from
her home region. Sons Enrico
and Daniele Camerucci play
hosts in the barrel-vaulted
dining room slung with
abstract oils by Rome-based
Spanish artist Maria Angeles.
Outstanding dishes include
a tortello (large ravioli-like
pasta) stuffed with ricotta
and a whole egg yolk, the
latter oozing out as you
break the pasta. The flan di
cipolla rossa (red-onion flan)
is delicate and delicious, as
is the soothing minestra al
sacco ('sack-style' soup),
its chewy cubes made of
compressed breadcrumbs,
parmesan and egg and
coloured with spinach or
tomato. On the vino front,
a leather-bound list offers
well-chosen wines from
across the country (ask for a
recommendation). Book at
least two days ahead.

4.

LOCAL TIP
Head to nostalgic,
wallet-friendly Er Buchetto
(Via del Viminale 2F)
for famed porchetta
sandwiches, washed
down with a beer or
tumbler of vino.

5.

5.

6.

PANELLA

Via Merulana 54
06 487 2435
http://panellaroma.com
Open Mon–Thurs 8am–11pm,
Fri–Sat 8am–12am,
Sun 8.30am–4pm

Some locals wryly call this bakery-cafe-provedore Bulgari, in reference to the prices. While it's not cheap, it's popular for good reason. In-house bakers roll out tray after tray of just-baked perfection, filling and refilling glass counters with succulent fruit tarts, fragrant biscotti and long wooden paddles laden with thin, crisp pizza al taglio (pizza by the slice). The latter is among the best in town. Lunch options also include trays of sautéed seasonal vegetables, golden arancini (rice balls) and other hot dishes, which you can combine for a customised lunch plate. The coffee is exceptional, and best ordered with a dollop of zabaglione cream, plonked straight into your brew. Much of the seating is at a long indoor communal bar table or on the alfresco terrace, with a few tables in the intimate back room where shelves are stocked with gourmet pantry goods. Order at the counter first, then grab a table.

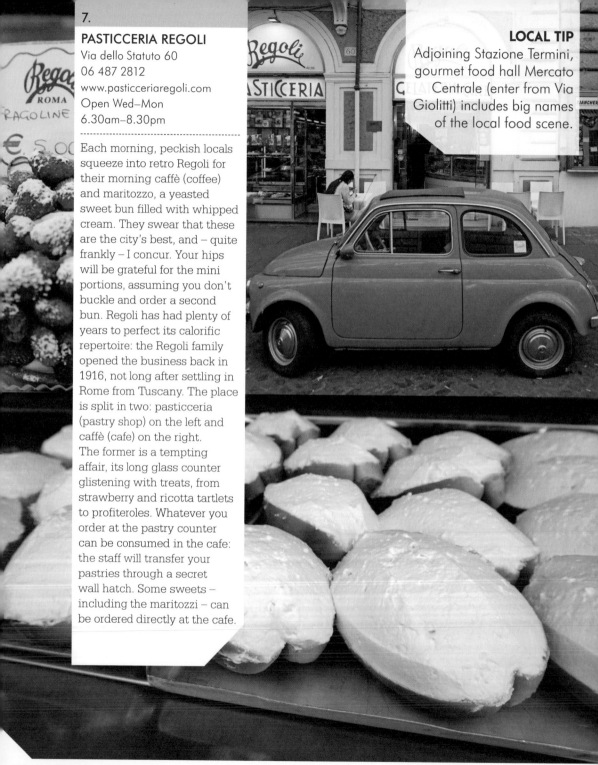

7.
PASTICCERIA REGOLI

Via dello Statuto 60
06 487 2812
www.pasticceriaregoli.com
Open Wed–Mon
6.30am–8.30pm

Each morning, peckish locals squeeze into retro Regoli for their morning caffè (coffee) and maritozzo, a yeasted sweet bun filled with whipped cream. They swear that these are the city's best, and – quite frankly – I concur. Your hips will be grateful for the mini portions, assuming you don't buckle and order a second bun. Regoli has had plenty of years to perfect its calorific repertoire: the Regoli family opened the business back in 1916, not long after settling in Rome from Tuscany. The place is split in two: pasticceria (pastry shop) on the left and caffè (cafe) on the right. The former is a tempting affair, its long glass counter glistening with treats, from strawberry and ricotta tartlets to profiteroles. Whatever you order at the pastry counter can be consumed in the cafe: the staff will transfer your pastries through a secret wall hatch. Some sweets – including the maritozzi – can be ordered directly at the cafe.

LOCAL TIP
Adjoining Stazione Termini, gourmet food hall Mercato Centrale (enter from Via Giolitti) includes big names of the local food scene.

8.

SALOTTO CARONTE
Via Machiavelli 23
06 700 1984
Open Mon–Fri 12pm–2am,
Sat 6.30pm–2am

A moody melange of dark-grey hues, industrial lamps and contemporary artworks, this cavernous bar and restaurant feels a world away from the gritty streets. While the restaurant has no shortage of fans, its globally influenced menu is hit-and-miss in my opinion. The bar-lounge is a better option: drop by early evening, when well-mixed drinks are accompanied by satisfying snacks. If you're lucky, you'll score one of the Chesterfield lounges, a suitable spot to sip a pre-dinner Spritzzone, a ginger-beer-spiked take on the aperitivo classic. A handful of wines are available by the glass, but it's the mixed drinks that shine. Gin fans will appreciate the handful of craft Italian options: order a G&T made with Sicilian Panarea, Tuscan Sabatini or Three Spirit's Piùcinque gin from the Veneto region. In case you're wondering about the bar's namesake, it's Charon, mythological ferryman of Hades responsible for carrying the souls of the recently deceased into the underworld. Thankfully, he's not offering rides out front.

A brilliant collection of ancient treasure awaits at the underrated **Palazzo Massimo alle Terme** (Largo di Villa Peretti 1). Highlights include bucolic 1st-century BCE frescoes from Villa Livia (the pad of Livia Drusilla, wife of Roman emperor Augustus), a 2nd-century-BCE Greek bronze statue of a pugilist, and the only known example of a mummified body from the Roman era.

Across the street lie the ruins of the **Terme di Diocleziano** (Viale Enrico de Nicola 78). Built between 298 and 306 CE, this was the largest public bathing complex in Rome, spanning 13 hectares and large enough to accommodate 3000 visitors at a time in its sprawl of thermal baths, pools, gymnasiums and libraries. Along with the Palazzo Altemps (see p. 045) and the Crypta Balbi (see p. 055), these two sites collectively make up the **Museo Nazionale Romano**; a combined ticket gives access to all four sites over three days.

Further south, the peak of **Esquiline Hill** – one of the seven original hills on which Rome was built – is crowned by the spectacular **Basilica di Santa Maria Maggiore** (Piazza Santa Maria Maggiore). The building is much older than its 18th-century Baroque facade, a fact attested to by its 14th-century belfry (Rome's tallest) and dazzling 5th- and 13th-century mosaics. This is the final resting place of Italian sculptor Pietro Bernini (creator of the Fontana della Barcaccia – a fountain depicting a sinking boat – at the foot of the Spanish Steps; see p. 081) and his much more famous son, Gian Lorenzo Bernini.

The basilica's altar reputedly contains the relics of St Matthew. Skip the Museo del Tesoro (Treasury Museum) for a guided tour of the basilica's 18th-century **Loggia delle Benedizioni**, which offers a close-up view of Filippo Rusuti's lustrous 13th-century mosaics. Tours of the loggia can be booked at the basilica's entrance.

Byzantine mosaics await inside the early 9th-century **Basilica di Santa Prassede** (Via Santa Prassede 9A), a short walk to the south. Complete with three naves, its most famous relic – stored in a glass case in the **Cappella di San Zenone** – is a piece of the column to which Christ was reputedly tied while being flogged. Its other treasures include the dazzling mosaics gracing the triumphal arch of the apse.

To the north-west, wretchedness, tragedy, sacrifice and love are also common themes at the lavish **Teatro dell'Opera di Roma** (Piazza Beniamino Gigli 1), which serves up world-class seasons of opera and ballet from September to June.

SAN LORENZO

Grungy, left-leaning San Lorenzo defies Rome's conservative, right-leaning image. A crumbling, tag-ridden grid of streets south-east of Termini train station, the district was developed in the early 20th century to house factory workers. Heavily bombed in World War II, it's now a gritty, post-industrial funk of street art, centri sociali (independent, semi-legal cultural centres) and late-night bars packed with beer-clutching students from the nearby university of La Sapienza.

Here, beauty is strictly in the detail, whether it be a piece of political stencil art, a soulful trattoria, or vintage factories turned into hidden galleries, ateliers, cafes and bistros.

24   JUN 80T6

SHOP
1 MYRIAM B
SHOP AND EAT
2 SAID

EAT
3 TRAM TRAM
4 PINSA E BUOI
5 KIKO SUSHI BAR
6 PASTIFICIO SAN LORENZO
EAT AND DRINK
7 IL SORI

SAN LORENZO

VERANO/DE LOLLIS

CIMITERO
DI CAMPO
VERANO

MUNICIPIO
IV

KIKO
SUSHI
BAR

PASTIFICIO
SAN LORENZO

VIA DE LOLLIS

VIA CESARE

VIA DEI DALMATI

VIA DEI

VIA DEI MARRUCINI

Chiesa
San Tommaso
Moro

Villa Mercede

SAID

MYRIAM B

RETI

VIA DEI VOLSCI

VIA DEI

SABELLI

Parco
dei Caduti
del 19 Luglio

VIA TIBURTINA

VIA DEI VOLSCI

VIA DEGLI SABELLI

VIA DEI PICENI

VIA

VIA DEI

VIA DEI SARDI

VIA DEGLI AUSONI

VIA DEI RETI

Hotel
Laurentia

Chiesa di
Santa Maria
Immacolata

IL SORÌ

VIA DEI LATINI

VIA DEGLI SABELLI

VIA DEI AURUNCI

VIA DEGLI APULI

VIA DEI

VIA DEI

VIA DEGLI ENOTRI

TRAM
TRAM

Parco
Sante de
Sanctis

SCALO S. LORENZO/
AUSONI

Piazza
dell'Immacolata

VIA MARSI

VIA DEGLI

VIA DEI CAMPANI

VIA DEI SARDI

Hotel Villa
San Lorenzo
Maria

TIBURTINO
QUARTIERE VI

SCALO S. LORENZO/
SARDI

VIA DI PORTA LABICANA

VIA DEI LUCANI

VIA SAN LORENZO

0   100 m

SCALO S. LORENZO/
TALAMO

N

VIA DEI BRUZI

PINSA
& BUOI

VIALE DELLO SCALO

CIRCONVALLAZIONE TIBURTINA

SCALO S. LORENZO

VIA GIOVANNI GIOLITTI

1.

MYRIAM B

Via degli Ausoni 7
06 4436 1305
www.myriamb.it
Open Mon 4.30–7.30pm,
Tues–Sat 11.30am–7.30pm

Hidden in an old pasta factory
turned arts hub, Myriam
Bottazzi's atelier showcases
boundary-breaking jewellery
design. Structured and highly
sculptural, her works have
graced the galleries of New
York's Museum of Art and
Design and are collected by
fans. A long-standing passion
for art, design and Japanese
aesthetic shapes the pieces,
many of which feature
unusual pairings of materials,
from metal and sequins, to
quartz with paillettes and
feathers. One necklace might
recall the twigs of a tree,
another fiery flames or a
black widow spider. There's a
powerful, primal feel to many
of her pieces. Myriam's small
collection of womenswear
is equally avant-garde, with
distinct details and fabrics
ranging from cotton and
organza to viscose with
metallic threading. In winter,
you can try on her fetching,
hand-painted gloves. Striking,
unconventional forms extend
to one-of-a-kind bags, which
might change shape or recall
strange sea creatures.

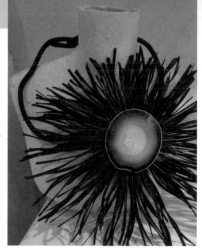

LOCAL TIP
Uniform outfitter
La Boutique del
Camice (Piazzale
Tiburtino 25–27)
stocks well-priced
casual garments,
from puffer vests and
jackets, to basic knits
and colourful aprons.

SAID

Via Tiburtina 135
06 446 9204
http://said.it
Open Tues–Thurs 10am–
12.30am, Fri 10am–1.30am,
Sat 11am–1.30am, Sun
11am–12.30am

Cocoa connoisseurs worship at this post-industrial temple to chocolate, suitably set in a chocolate factory from 1923. Vintage machinery, scales and moulds decorate the shop and cafe, its counters neatly lined with some of the city's finest pralines and truffles. These are chocolates that taste just like their given flavour, whether that's rosemary, cinnamon, chilli or – my undisputed favourite – cardamom. If you like your chocolate nutty, check out the glass jars on the shelves, filled with slabs of dark, milk and white chocolate laced with generous amounts of pistachios and almonds. The cafe serves a suitably fine cioccolata calda (hot chocolate), as well as decent coffee and flaky, breakfast-friendly cornetti (Italian croissants). While the space also incorporates a restaurant, you're better off sticking to the cafe and its divine chocolate creations.

3.

TRAM TRAM

Via dei Reti 46
06 49 04 16
www.tramtram.it
Open Tues–Sun 12.30–
3.30pm & 7.30–11pm (closed
Sun & open Mon July & Aug)

Against the rattle of passing trams, octogenarian Rosanna di Vittoria and daughters Fabiola and Antonella serve up fresh, honest home-cooking at their lovingly worn corner trattoria. The menu straddles Roman and Puglian influences, which translates into dishes such as comforting coda alla vaccinara (Roman oxtail stew), fava-bean purée with bitter chicory, or a rich, flavour-packed tortino di alici (anchovy tart) jammed with artichokes, raisins, pine nuts and dehydrated cherry tomatoes. Pasta dishes include some interesting options; if it's on offer, don't pass up the pasta with broccoli and clams, one of Tram Tram's greatest hits. The wooden dining tables date back to the 1940s, while both the tram plaques and bench are original. One of the few things that have changed over the years is the crowd, the old, card-playing workers now mostly replaced by food lovers, artists, professors and protégés. Book a day or two ahead if heading in for dinner later in the week.

4.

PINSA & BUOI

Viale dello Scalo
San Lorenzo 15–17
06 445 6640
www.pinsaebuoiristorante.com
Open Mon–Sun 12–11.30pm

According to the Roman poet Virgil, the Trojan hero Aeneas tucked into a pinsa upon landing in Lavinio, south of Rome. Millennia later, modern Romans have rediscovered the joys of this oval-shaped flatbread, the ancient forefather of pizza. This wood-panelled hideaway, perched at the southern tip of San Lorenzo ferments its dough – a combination of soft-grain, rice and soy flours – for two to three days, resulting in a wonderfully light texture with a crisp, charred finish. Toppings cover all corners of the country, from deep-south staples like Sicilian anchovies and Calabrian 'nduja (a spicy spreadable salami) to northern speck and gorgonzola, to die-hard Roman combos like pecorino romano, guanciale (cured pig's cheek) and egg. The best way to decide is over a tagliere di salumi e formaggi (platter of cured meats and cheeses), a showcase of DOC-designated and Slow Food–approved edibles. Book ahead, especially later in the week.

5.

KIKO SUSHI BAR

Piazzale del Verano 90–91
06 9484 9822
www.kikosushibar.it
Open Tues–Sun 1–2.30pm &
8–11pm

Sleek, minimalist Kiko seems an unlikely bedfellow for grungy San Lorenzo, but then some of the best relationships are also the oddest. Lording over the sushi bar is Tokyo expat Kikuchi Atsufumi, wearing wooden geta (traditional Japanese footwear) and slicing up some of the city's finest raw-fish morsels. From the toro (tuna belly) and hotate (scallop) to the sake (salmon) and uni (sea urchin), the sashimi here is excellent: super fresh and silky. The various maki sushi (sushi rolls) are also satisfying, with combinations such as tuna with flying-fish roe and avocado, or salmon and avocado in a spicy sauce. Least impressive are the nigiri, in which the rice dominates. The menu's supporting cast includes golden tempura and a cleansing insalata di alghe (seaweed salad). My friends and I routinely conclude meals with sublime gelato flavoured with ginger, green tea and (my personal favourite) black sesame. Sushi-bar seating makes this place an appealing option for solo diners. Book ahead.

LOCAL TIP
Vinyl hunters sift the racks at Transmission (Via dei Salentini 27), where the mostly second-hand stock includes some interesting, rare finds.

6.

PASTIFICIO SAN LORENZO

Via Tiburtina 196
06 9727 3519
www.pastificiosanlorenzo.com
Open Mon–Fri 12.30–3pm &
7pm–2am, Sat 7pm–2am

When your address is a factory-turned-arts incubator, one expects a little creative verve. In the case of the Pastificio, it's evident in the stacked art tomes, framed photographs by greats like Hungarian-Italian Ghitta Carell, and the eclectic splash of vintage furniture (including an old gym bar turned into a bar stool). Sink into a velvety sofa for a calming glass of vino, or slide into one of the diner-like booths for creative dishes such as Sicilian prawn tartare with refreshing puntarelle (Catalonian chicory), panko-crumbed fried anchovies with artichoke cream, or a vegan tofu burger with prized onions from Tropea in Calabria. The bread, ketchup and mayo are made in-house, and the barkeeps mix a decent cocktail. Squint hard enough and you might just think you're lounging in Tribeca, New York City.

7.

IL SORÌ
Via dei Volsci 51
393 4318681
http://www.ilsori.it
Open Mon–Sat 5.30pm–2am

In studenty San Lorenzo,
Il Sorì is a drinking hole for
grown-ups. The wines are
thoughtfully chosen, well
priced and predominantly
Italian, with the odd French
or Spanish offering for good
measure. The bar counter is
at the back of the intimate
space, and it's here – in
the light of a bottle-turned-
table-lamp – that I prefer to
perch myself, chatting with
the staff about vino, politics
or temperamental Roman
weather. Wines aside, the
place offers simple bites that
showcase ingredients from
smaller, artisanal producers.
You might find smoked-
tuna tartare with pine
nuts and raisins, sausages
with friarielli (bitter greens)
or even Gallic rillettes de
porc (French pork rillettes).
Seating is limited, so head
in before 7pm if you're after
a table.

Although San Lorenzo lacks big-ticket attractions, it's not without its cultural assets. At the neighbourhood's north-eastern edge stands the beautiful **Basilica di San Lorenzo Fuori le Mura** (Piazzale San Lorenzo), built on the burial site of 3rd-century Christian martyr St Lawrence. The original church was constructed by Constantine in the 4th century before being rebuilt in the 6th and again in the 13th century. Although altered further over the ensuing centuries, heavy damage during World War II air raids saw it restored to its 13th-century appearance. The medieval frescoes decorating the portico depict events from the lives of St Lawrence and St Stephen. The basilica's mosaic tiles are attributed to Jacopo the Younger, a member of the revered Cosmati family of sculptors and architects. Interestingly, the basilica is also the final resting place of Italy's 30th prime minister, Alcide De Gasperi, considered a founding father of the European Union.

Sprawling beside the church is the **Cimitero di Campo Verano** (Piazzale del Verano 1). Rome's largest cemetery, its sweep of heartbroken marble angels and proud mausoleums makes for a strangely moving, evocative wander.

For something altogether more contemporary, drop by San Lorenzo's **Fondazione Pastificio Cerere** (Via degli Ausoni 7), a former pasta factory turned contemporary art hub housing exhibition spaces and studios, such as designer Myriam B (see p. 198).

SAN LORENZO LOCAL RECOMMENDS

Lorna Davidson is a self-proclaimed 'social butterfly' and part of The Roman Guy, a tour company offering a modern and tasty spin on Rome.

Pinsa & Buoi (*see* p. 200) is one of the best places to get your hands on 'pinsa', a pizza-type dish that dates back to Ancient Rome. The homemade gnocchi is also not to be missed.

Said (*see* p. 199) is perfect as a relaxed afternoon hangout. It's one of the few cafe-style venues in Rome where you're free to sit for a couple of hours and chat with friends or locals.

Cimitero di Campo Verano (*see* p. 206) is an evocative spot to walk off your lunch. While doing so, seek out the headstone of legendary *La dolce vita* actor Marcello Mastroianni.

Tram Tram (*see* p. 200) is where I order risotto with mussels and sit by the window to watch Rome's retro trams pass by. Don't expect a sign reading 'Tram Tram' on the exterior; just look for number 46.

Street art from celebrated local and international artists adorns San Lorenzo. Alice Pasquini's work dominates on Via dei Sabelli, revealing a more modern creative side to Rome that many don't realise exists.

Pigneto is Rome's inked, pierced hipster. Once crime-ridden and drug-addled, the neighbourhood has found its salvation in craft beer, sleeve tattoos and politically charged street art. On and around car-free Via del Pigneto, eclectic bars and bistros lure artists, students and hip young families for nightly aperitivo sessions, locavore dining or long, lazy weekend brunches.

Speckled with old workers' cottages and private gardens, these streets have appeared in a string of classic Italian films, mostly notably *Accattone*, Pier Paolo Pasolini's tale of thieves, pimps and prostitutes. From Pigneto's northern edge, car-jammed Via Prenestina shoots east into concrete-block suburbs and unexpected dining gems.

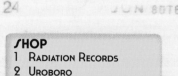

24   JUN 8076

SHOP
1 Radiation Records
2 Uroboro

EAT
3 Waraku
4 Mazzo
5 So What?!?
6 Pigneto Quarantuno
7 Rosti al Pigneto

EAT AND DRINK
8 La Santeria
9 La Santeria di Mare

PIGNETO
AND AROUND

TIBURTINO
QUARTIERE VI

TO WARAKU
& MAZZO
(SEE MAP LEFT)
➡

Parco del
Torrione
Prenestino

Mausoleo
detto
'Il Torrione'
(ruins)

VIA MONTECUCCOLI

VIA ETTORE FIERAMOSCA

VIA SCIPIONE

VIA RIVERA

VIA PRENESTINA

VIA RAIMONDO

PRENESTINA/
OFFICINE ATAC

P.LE PRENESTINO

PRENESTINA/
GIOVENALE

Teatro
Sala
Vignoli

Chiesa
San
Leone

RADIATION
RECORDS

VIA L'AQUILA

VIA ASCOLI PICENO

VIA MACERATA

VIA PERUGIA

VIA CASILINA

CIRCONVALLAZIONE CASILINA

VIA BARTOLOMEO D'ALVIANO

VIA FANFULLA DA LODI

VIA GIOVANNI BRANCALEONE

VIA ETTORE GIOVENALE

VIA ROMANELLO DA FORLI

2501
MURAL

PICCOLA
MARIA
MURAL

MAUPAL'S
EYE
MURAL

UROBORO

IO SONO I NOMI MURAL

SO WHAT?!?

PIGNETO
QUARANTUNO

VIA BRACCIO DA MONTONE

NECCI DAL 1924

SPIRITO

FLAVIO
SOLO
MURAL

LUCA
ZAMOC
MURAL

ROSTI AL PIGNETO

VIA GROSSETO

VIA FIVIZZANO

VIA CASILINA

CIRCONVALLAZIONE CASILINA

VIA DEL PIGNETO

PIGNETO

LA SANTERIA DI MARE
LA SANTERIA

Chiesa di
Sant'Elena

2501
MURAL

VIA ADRIANO

VIA BALBI

S. ELENA

VIA LUIGI FILIPPO DE MAGISTRIS

CIRCONVALLAZIONE CASILINA

PRENESTINO
LABICANO
QUARTIERE VII

VIA GIOVANNI DE AGOSTINI

VIA CRISTOFORO BUONDELMONTI

VECCHIA

AQUA
CLAUDIO

VIA CASILINA

MUNICIPIO V

Piazza
Tolomeo

VIA DI VILLA SERVENTI

VIA DELLA STAZIONE TUSCOLANA

VIA CASILINA VECCHIA

N

0   100 m

VILLINI

209

1.

RADIATION RECORDS
Via Romanello da Forlì 14
06 9028 6578
http://shop.radiationrecords.net
Open Mon–Fri 10.30am–2pm
& 4–8pm, Sat 10.30am–8pm

On Friday and Saturday evenings, Radiation can feel more like a block party than a record shop, its small army of regulars here to hang out, banter with owner Marco Sannino and riffle through crates packed with new and pre-loved discs. You'll find a solid selection of indie, punk, new wave and rock records, as well as soul, funk, reggae and jazz. On top of this is a booty of CDs and cassette tapes, band-themed tees, music-themed books (several in English), as well as kooky gifts – think Sex Pistols coffee mugs and *Abbey Road*–themed jigsaw puzzles. Bargain hunters will always find a stack or three on sale, and the place also hosts live music every fortnight or so; see Radiation's Facebook page for upcoming gigs. If you're in town on the third weekend in April, don't miss their World Record Store Day shindig, a cult event famed for its sales, in-store gigs and collectable, limited-edition picture discs, released annually to mark the event.

UROBORO
Via Ascoli Piceno 21
06 6485 1272
Open Tues–Fri 12–9pm,
Sat 3–10pm, Sun 5–10pm

Inked skin inspires this most intriguing of independent bookshops. Its collection offers a wide, thoughtful selection of illustrated and photographic books on the tattoo, its history, styles and various inspirations. This means you're as likely to find a coveted tome on anatomy, medieval engravings or Caravaggio as you are on classic American tattoos. Scan the shelves and you might also stumble upon harder-to-find titles exploring botanical illustrations, ukiyo-e (Japanese woodblock prints) or subway art. Many books are in English and produced by smaller, niche publishers, with some titles self-published by tattoo artists themselves. Uroboro also stocks limited-edition tattoo-art prints, as well as locally printed t-shirts and totes. Its basement space is used to host a range of special gigs, from exhibitions to book launches. Check the Facebook page or Instagram for upcoming events.

3.

WARAKU

Via Prenestina 321
06 2170 2358
Open Tues 8–10.30pm,
Wed–Sun 12.30–2.30pm &
8–10.30pm

Japanophile Maurizio Di
Stefano started his ramen
joint as a pop-up at the back
of a gym. As word caught
on, so did the need for a
larger space. His restaurant
is a narrow, homely space
decorated with original
Japanese artworks and a
giant street-art mural by
local tattoo artist Funkamore.
Maurizio honed his skills in
Japan under the guidance
of his wife Miwako's uncle.
Waraku's noodles are made
the old-school way, and the
menu's long list of ramen
dishes spans the traditional
and the tweaked. If you can't
decide between classic shoyu
ramen, Thai-style ramen or
nutty, intense tantanmen
ramen with spicy pork,
Maurizio is usually on hand
to guide you. Other Japanese
classics include made-from-
scratch gyoza (dumplings),
okonomiyaki (savoury
Japanese pancake), hot
and cold soba noodles, and
crunchy karaage (Japanese
fried chicken). For dessert
try a matcha tiramisu, and
quench your thirst with
unfiltered Japanese beer or,
my favourite, genmaicha
(toasted brown-rice green
tea). Oishii!

4.

MAZZO

Via delle Rose 54
06 6496 2847
www.thefooders.it/mazzo
Open Mon–Fri 6pm–12am,
Sat 1–3.30pm & 6pm–12am

It may be tiny, but 12-seater
Mazzo has accrued an epic
reputation. The restaurant's
single communal table
draws food lovers from
across the city to swoon
over simple takes on Roman
soul food. Causing the stir
are young chefs and couple
Francesca Barreca and Marco
Baccanelli, who champion
local, organic produce
(much of it from friends'
farms) in dishes such as
wholemeal tonnarelli pasta
with snails and peperoni
cruschi (crunchy peppers),
or tender trippa fritta (fried
tripe) in a tomato and mint
sauce. The recipe for Mazzo's
juicy polpette (meatballs) –
laced with pecorino cheese,
garlic and parsley – is from
Francesca's own nonna
(grandmother). The clued-
up vibe extends to the list
of natural wines from small
producers. Curiously, the
place also has a soft spot for
gin, including lesser-known
drops such as Solo Wild
Gin from Sardinia. Mazzo
has two dinner sittings, at
8pm and 10pm: always book
ahead. For a super-local and
relaxed vibe, lunch here on
a Saturday.

4.

3.

3.

5.

SO WHAT?!?
Via Ettore Giovenale 56
329 8265250
www.sowhatvegan.com
Open Mon & Wed–Fri 7.30pm–
12am, Sat–Sun 12.30–3pm &
7.30pm–12am

Don't be fooled by the belligerent name: So What?!? is a chilled, affable beast at heart. Decked out in B-grade film posters, toy robots and brightly coloured chairs, it's the passion project of vegan chef Paolo Petralia and his partner Alessandra. The duo dishes up comforting plant-based dishes that burst with flavour. Their menu offers meat-free interpretations of numerous classic Italian dishes, from crespella di farro bio con tofu (organic spelt-flour crepe filled with spinach and tofu) to fettucine al ragù di seitan (fettucine pasta in a wheat-gluten ragout). The star dish is polpette che la nonna non ti ha mai fatto (meatballs that your grandmother has never made you), cooked slightly crisp on the outside and wonderfully moist and succulent inside. Opt for the original version, served in a vibrant sugo di pomodoro (tomato sauce). Libations include craft beers and vegan wines, the latter hailing from the Lazio region.

LOCAL TIP
For outdoor drinks in a garden setting, hit buzzy Necci dal 1924 (Via Fanfulla da Lodi 68), former hangout of film director Pier Paolo Pasolini.

LOCAL TIP

For cocktails (and a game of roulette at the bar) try speakeasy drinking hole Spirito (Via Fanfulla da Lodi 53) – reservations recommended.

PIGNETO QUARANTUNO

Via del Pigneto 41
06 7039 9483
www.pignetoquarantuno.it
Open Mon & Sat 5.30pm–2am, Tues–Fri 5pm–2am,
Sun 11.30am–2am

There's something reassuringly comforting about Pigneto Quarantuno, one of the neighbourhood's best-loved trattorias (casual restaurant). It's dressed with simple timber tables, paper placemats and beautiful stemware, and the menu is a tribute to seasonal Roman classics and in-house creativity. The focaccia makes for a promising prologue, while stand-out primi (first courses) include cacio e pepe (pasta with pecorino romano and cracked pepper). Request a mezza porzione (half portion) to leave room for secondi (mains), such as perfectly cooked fillet of baccalà (salted cod) with olives and savoy cabbage. The wine list is decent if not thrilling, with an ample selection of local Lazio reds and a small number of drops by the glass. If it's on the menu, promise me you'll wrap up with the fluffy ricotta cream with raisins, hazelnuts, rum and rich chocolate sauce – I drool at the thought of it. When the kitchen closes, the place becomes a local drinking den.

7.

ROSTI AL PIGNETO

Via Bartolomeo d'Alviano 65
06 275 2608
www.rostialpigneto.it
Open Mon–Sun 9am–1am

Casual, modern Rosti is a darling of the Sunday brunch scene, its large front garden and verandah a huge hit with everyone from young families with hyperactive kids to hip gay couples. Brunch (€20 per head) is of the buffet variety: grab a plate and make your way along the central table laden with dishes, from antipasti to dessert. There's a generous selection of vegetables and other contorni (side dishes), along with a number of cheeses. The choice of primi (first courses) and secondi (mains) is more limited, with rotating options such as ricotta and spinach ravioli, pasta al forno con salsiccia (pasta bake with sausage) or stinco di maiale (pork shank). Sweet tooths happily laden their plates with fruit and nut crostate (tarts), cakes and muffins, but the tiramisu fails to impress most locals. During the week, there's a short breakfast menu, lunch buffet, and evening burgers, salads and Neapolitan-style pizza. Book Sunday brunch at least three days ahead.

LA SANTERIA

Via del Pigneto 213
06 6480 1606
Open Mon–Sun 6.30pm–1am

Will you swill the Sardinian cannonau Renosu or the Ligurian vermentino malvasia? Quirky, neighbourly La Santeria throws up some serious conundrums. Thankfully, wine by the glass averages a palatable €5 to €6 so you don't have to play favourites. Scan the blackboard for the day's edit of wines, commonly featuring natural drops from lesser-known talents such as Lazio boys Sete. If you prefer hops over grape, craft Italian beers are available on tap. Compact, softly lit and decked out in vintage mirrors and offbeat art, the wine bar also serves solid graze-friendly bites. Choose from juicy buffalo mozzarella and prized Cetara anchovies to pagnotelle alla romana (traditional round panini) and the rarely found scarpetta, a Jewish-Roman pita-style sandwich. If you're undecided on fillings, follow the locals and request it with coda alla vaccinara (Roman oxtail stew). There's a scattering of tables, but I like to perch at the long marble bar, where you can chat with the barkeep and eye the cockatoo figurine.

LA SANTERIA DI MARE

Via del Pigneto 209
06 8923 0730
Open Mon–Sun 6.30pm–2am

Life is infinitely better with freshly shucked oysters and bubbles, and both are on the menu at the seafood-centric sibling of La Santeria (*see* p. 217). The range of oysters – mostly French – rotates regularly, and is accompanied by a repertoire of fresh fish and simple seafood dishes. The classic charcuterie plate gets a coastal makeover with the salumi di mare e crudi, a trio of bites that might include tuna tartare with spicy 'nduja (spreadable Calabrian salami made with pork, roasted peppers and spices) and sumac; house-smoked pesce spada (swordfish) and fig jam on crisp pane genovese (Genovese-style bread); and herb-crusted tuna steak. Like La Santeria, the restaurant serves pagnotelle (traditional soft-bread sandwiches), scarpette (pita-style sandwiches) plus well-priced natural wines. The interior attests to owner Gioia Di Paolo's love of all things vintage, but on warmer nights the place to be is the bulb-strung garden. The kitchen usually closes at 11.30pm, after which the space transforms into a cocktail bar.

Pigneto and neighbouring Torpignattara to the east are fertile grounds for street art. Paste-ups are prolific on and off Via del Pigneto, especially the stretch between the elevated Circonvallazione Tiburtina and Via Giovanni Brancaleone. Check out the **pop-style mural by local Flavio Solo** on the corner of Via del Pigneto and Via Fivizzano, then continue east along Via del Pigneto, crossing the railway bridge and turning left (north) into Circonvallazione Casilina.

Two blocks away, Via Fortebraccio is dominated by a soaring **abstract mural by Milanese artist 2501**. One block south of the railway bridge, Via Luigi Filippo De Magistris 15 features a second mural by the artist. In case you're wondering, the arches to the south of Circonvallazione Casilina are

the **Aqua Claudio**, an ancient Roman aqueduct begun by Emperor Caligula in 38 CE and completed by Emperor Claudius in 52 CE.

Back on Via del Pigneto, Roman legend is the focus of Modenese artist **Luca Zamoc's epic mural** above Pigneto metro station. The piece was commissioned to coincide with the Season 6 launch of popular Netflix series *Suburra*. Running north from Via del Pigneto, Via Fanfulla da Lodi features a series of murals related to neo-realist Italian film director Pier Paolo Pasolini. These include **Io sono i nomi** (I Am the Names) by artist Omino 71 at number 49, Mr Klevra's veiled young woman (known as **Piccola Maria**) at number 56, and Maupal's **Eye**, an intense depiction of an eye at number 43.

Further east in the Torpignattara district, the corner of Via del Pigneto and Via Lodovico Pavoni is home to Rome's tallest mural, the 32-metre-high **Coffee Break**. It's the work of Polish duo Etam Cru (Sainer and Bezt), who added the coffee motif as a tribute to local residents who kindly offered them coffee while they executed the piece. Nearby are two other standout murals: Swedish artist Etnik's colourful **cubes** on Via Bartolomeo Perestrello (between Via Lodovico Pavoni and Via Antonio Tempesta) and, directly opposite on Via Antonio Tempesta, Spanish artist Dulk's spaced-out red **panda**.

If your cravings for street art haven't yet waned, walk south along Via Antonio Tempesta, cross Via Casalina, and continue south on Via Gabrio Serbelloni.

The side of number 60 features a mural of **Tom Sawyer** by prolific French artist Jef Aérosol, considered a pioneer of the street-art movement. Around the corner, fellow Frenchman C251 engages with his **bearded man and feline** at Via Ciro da Urbino 12–16, while the giant **technicolor mural** on the corner of Via Ciro da Urbino and Via di Tor Pignattara is the work of Peruvian-born artist Carlos Atoche.

Fashionable professionals, hotspot-seeking food lovers and university types fawn over Salario, a vibrant middle-class pocket where the living is good and camera-wielding tourists are few and far between. Here, veteran lighting shops, cobblers and market stalls mix it up with dynamic bistros, third-wave coffee and modern art, rousing the ever-growing interest of cool-hunters seeking the next big thing.

Across leafy Viale Regina Margherita and its steady stream of cars, trams, suited folk and window shoppers lies equally comfortable Trieste, home to Quartiere Coppedè and its wonderfully kooky collection of early 20th-century architecture.

24   JUN 8876

*SHOP
1 CASTIGLIONI
2 TORREFAZIONE ENOTECA
   GIOVANNI DE *SANCTIS

17

EAT
3 MARZAPANE
4 GRUÉ
5 PANIS 1890
EAT AND DRINK
6 FARO

*SALARIO AND TRIE*STE

LIEGI/
BELLINI

BLUE
MARLIN
& CO.

Grand
Hotel
Beverly
Hills

PANIS 1890

TORREFAZIONE
ENOTECA
GIOVANNI
DE SANCTIS

Chiesa di
San Saturnino

0   100 m

N

QUARTIERE
COPPEDÈ

PIAZZA MINCIO
& FONTANA
DELLE RANE

TRIESTE
QUARTIERE XVII

Piazza
Trasimeno

Santa Maria
Addolorata

Piazza
Buenos
Aires

BUENOS AIRES

GRUÉ

MUNICIPIO II

Santa
Maria della
Merce de
e Sant'Adriano
Martire

Villa
Albani

Hotel
Albani

Piazza
Dalmazia

CASTIGLIONI
CASTIGLIONI

CASTIGLIONI

Parco di
Villa Albani

V.LE REGINA
MARGHERITA/
NIZZA

LUMA

Piazza Regina
Margherita

SALARIO
QUARTIERE IV

MUSEO D'ARTE
CONTEMPORANEA
DI ROMA
(MACRO)

MARZAPANE

V.LE REGINA
MARGHERITA/
NOMENTANA

RIGASÙ

Hotel
Fiume

Cinema Savoy

Piazza
Alessandria

Hotel
Porta
Pia

Piazza
Fiume

Mercato
Nomentano

Cinema
Europa

Chiesa del
Corpus
Domini

FARO

Piazzale
di Porta
Pia

1.

CASTIGLIONI

Corso Trieste 23B
06 4425 0937
www.castiglionidal1927.it
Open Mon 4–8pm, Tues–Sat
10.30am–1.30pm & 4.30–8pm

Vintage outfitter Castiglioni
has been smartening Roman
wardrobes since 1927.
Established by Vincenzo
Castiglioni (that's him in
the photographs on the
wall), it's now run by his
granddaughter, Claudia.
Complete with in-house tailor,
the shop sells everything
needed for a classic Italian
look, from dashing suits,
jackets and trenches, to
beautifully tailored shirts,
cashmere scarves and pure
Merino-wool gloves. While
Castiglioni produces much
of what's on the racks and in
the vintage glass counters,
you'll also find Duca Visconti
di Modrone corduroys,
Paolo Da Ponte braces and
Bugatti socks, as well as
Italian leather brogues, fedora
hats and cufflinks. Prices
are reasonable for the high
quality, with suits starting
at around €170. Women's
clothing and accessories are
also available. There are two
other branches nearby: Viale
Regina Margherita 149, aimed
at a younger market, and
Viale Regina Margherita 165,
whose focus is sartorial.

LOCAL TIP
For men's and women's
threads with a subtle
vintage, Americana feel,
pop into long-standing
fashion favourite Blue
Marlin & Co (Viale Regina
Margherita 12–14).

2

LOCAL TIP
Hole-in-the-wall Da Agostino (Corso Trieste 66) is a local favourite for fresh, flavour-packed pizza al taglio (pizza by the slice).

TORREFAZIONE ENOTECA GIOVANNI DE SANCTIS
Via Tagliamento 88
06 855 2287
Open Mon–Sat
9am–1.30pm & 4–8pm

Time stands perfectly still inside this vintage neighbourhood coffee roaster and providore, owned and operated by the De Sanctis family since 1924. Everything from the front door and counters to the soaring wooden shelves are original, the latter suitably topped with old coffee and liqueur tins. Indeed, the business is as old as the building itself. You'll find freshly roasted coffee blends, a good selection of bottled vino (many from smaller wine producers), and take-home treats for a proper Italian pantry makeover. Snoop through my own shopping bag and you're likely to find jars of Calabrian sughetto (sauce), cans of high-quality Sardanelli tuna, and perhaps a bag or two of speciality rice from Piedmont's Cascina Veneria. Chances are you'll also find a few Venchi chocolates or a packet of biscotti from Sicilian pasticceria (pastry shop) Fratelli Scimeca. Prepare to take a few pics: this is one of the city's most endearing historical shops.

3.

MARZAPANE

Via Velletri 39
06 6478 1692
www.marzapaneroma.com
Open Tues 8–11pm, Wed–Sun
1–3pm & 8–11pm

She may be Spanish, but chef Alba Esteve Ruiz serves up an incredible carbonara. A superbly creamy and decadent dish, its secret is the generous use of egg yolk and 14-month aged pecorino – and I suspect the five-month cured guanciale (cured pig's cheek) and mature parmesan play their role too. Not that Marzapane is your classic Roman trattoria. Clean lines, Nordic furniture and a neutral interior palette set a subdued, contemporary scene, while the menu marries Italian tradition with modern, global creativity. This might mean guinea-fowl tortelli paired with stilton, baccalà (salted cod) served with a Basque pil-pil fish sauce, or delicate amberjack cooked with kefir, a fermented milk drink originating in the Caucasus Mountains. Alba's past gigs include a stint at Girona's triple-Michelin-starred restaurant El Celler de Can Roca. From Wednesday to Friday there are good-value 'light lunch' degustation menus (€30), four-course affairs focused on either meat or seafood dishes. Reservations are sensible.

4.

GRUÉ

Viale Regina Margherita 95
06 841 2220
www.gruepasticceria.it
Open Sun–Fri 7am–9pm

Dynamic and talented pair Marta Boccanera and Felice Venanzi have taken the Roman pasticceria to dizzying heights with Grué. An airy, contemporary pastry shop and cafe, its rows of pastries, cakes and chocolates are veritable artworks. The couple pours endless hours of research into every creation and boldly experiments to create knockout versions of classic treats as well as original concoctions. Pretty much everything is made from scratch in-house. Once you've taken a photo, sink your teeth into must-try pastries such as granata (cocoa shortbread with a cream of raspberry, chocolate and cherry liqueur) or the Sacher, a dark-chocolate and almond Sacher biscuit with chocolate ganache and apricot jam. Don't overlook the pralines, in flavours such as mandarino (mandarin), arachide salato (salted peanut) and finocchietto (fennel). The cafe also serves high-quality savouries. In the evenings, locals head in for aperitivo, where €8 lands you a cocktail and a small selection of devilishly good canapés.

5.

PANIS 1890
Via Tagliamento 62
06 841 7029
Open Mon–Sat 7am–8pm

Mention Biscotti Gentilini to a Roman and you're likely to kindle a nostalgic smile. The sweet, dry biscuits were once made and sold at this very site, now home to busy Panis 1890. The original Gentilini bakery counter now hangs high above the current glass versions, where baked treats include glorious crostate (tarts), occhi di bue (round shortbread biscuits with a sweet jam centre), and caprese al limone (a lemon-spiked twist on Capri's famous almond and white chocolate cake). If it's lunchtime, squeeze inside for wonderful, just-out-of-the-oven pizza al taglio (pizza by the slice), dressed with toppings such as salsiccia e cicoria (pork sausage and chicory) or carciofo, pomodorino e rucola (artichoke, cherry tomato and rocket). The fourth-generation bakery also stocks jars of heavenly, pectin-free fruit jams from the Monastero Trappiste di Vitorchiano, esteemed supplier of the Vatican pantry.

6.

FARO
Via Piave 55
06 4281 5714
www.farorome.com
Open Mon–Fri 7am–5pm, Sat
8am–5pm, Sun 9am–5pm

Rome's first speciality coffee shop is helmed by young, easy-going Dario Fociani, whose passion for third wave coffee culture was first sparked while working in Melbourne. After honing his skills at top cafes and micro-roasteries in London and Berlin, he opened his own new-school coffee shop in the Italian capital, determined to gently convert locals from the heavily roasted, commercial espresso they know. The space itself is upbeat, casual and convivial, with solid timber tables, trailing ivy and killer tunes on the sound system. Slurp from a rotating cast of coffees, showcasing top European artisanal roasters such as Italy's Gardelli, Denmark's April and La Cabria, and Berlin's The Barn and Five Elephant. Brewing techniques include espresso, V60 and Aeropress, while the moreish pastries are made by local artisan baker Rami Kosman, his own mentor none other than renowned Italian pastry chef Luigi Biasetto. Listed on wooden clipboards, lunch bites change according to the morning's best produce.

Pre-book your ticket online (www.galleriaborghese.beniculturali.it) to visit the **Museo e Galleria Borghese** (Piazzale Scipione Borghese 5), located just to the west of Salario. The gallery houses one of Europe's most extraordinary collections of art, the legacy of ruthless art collector Cardinal Scipione Borghese.

Salario is home to the **Museo d'Arte Contemporanea di Roma** (Via Nizza 138). Nicknamed MACRO, it's a top-tier spot for exhibitions of contemporary Italian and international art. The gallery's permanent collection – which spans the 1960s to the early 2000s – includes works from a long list of Italian heavyweights, including Mimmo Rotella, Carla Accardi and Mario Schifano. MACRO's architecture is a worthy drawcard too – the building is a converted Peroni brewery reimagined by radical French architect Odile Decq.

Trieste's most worthy drawcard is the **Quartiere Coppodè**. Best entered through the archway on the corner of Via Tagliamento and Via Dora, the compact residential estate – built between 1913 and 1926 – was the brainchild of esoteric Florentine architect Gino Coppedè. Its gleeful mishmash of frescoed facades, Moorish arches, medieval-style turrets, Art Nouveau sculptures and gargoyles seem to be pulled straight out of a fairytale. The quartiere is anchored by Piazza Mincio and its adorable **Fontana delle Rane** (Fountain of the Frogs), a modern spin on the Ghetto's famous Renaissance-era **Fontana delle Tartarughe** (Turtle Fountain; *see* p. 055).

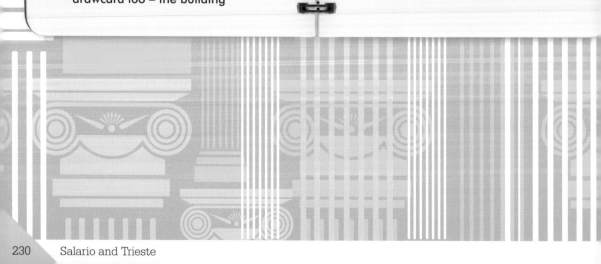

Barbara Lessona is a well-seasoned fashion PR identity and runs a concierge service for visitors to Rome, specialising in bespoke shopping tours. Local artisans and interior decoration are her passions.

Grué (*see* p. 226) has an amazing kitchen creating exceptional edibles. The mini-sized pastries offer modern takes on traditional recipes, and the Sunday à-la-carte lunch menu is always different and fun.

Torrefazione Enoteca Giovanni de Sanctis (*see* p. 225) has been run by the same family since the 1950s. The original timber fittings are beautiful and everything from the marmalades to the Sicilian liqueurs are unique.

Castiglioni (*see* p. 224) is a local institution, selling classic 'Made in Italy' clothes and accessories for men and women, from wool and cashmere sweaters, to overcoats and suits. The hats and gloves are exceptional.

Rigasù (Via Nomentana 135) is fabulous for a wardrobe refresh. You'll find well-priced, ready-to-wear dresses, blouses, trousers, knitwear, accessories and shoes, including Italian winter boots. The costume jewellery is by local artisans.

Luma (Via Alessandria 210) is an amazing, tiny, in-the-know shoe store. From France's Robert Clergerie to high-end Italian artisans, this is La La Land for fashion lovers. If you're after that one special pair, look no further.

GETTING TO & FROM FIUMICINO AIRPORT

Leonardo Da Vinci airport, commonly referred to as Fiumicino, is Rome's main international airport, 30 kilometres south-west of central Rome. Options for getting to and from the airport include the following:

Leonardo Express Train

Express trains run between Fiumicino and Stazione Termini, Rome's main train station. Tickets can be purchased using cash or card from station ticket-vending machines and cost €14 one way. Journey time is 32 minutes. Trains run every 15 to 30 minutes between 6.23am and 11.23pm from the airport and between 5.35am and 10.35pm from Termini.

FL1 Commuter Train

Slower commuter trains connect Fiumicino to Roma-Trastevere, Roma-Ostiense and Roma-Tiburtina stations. From the airport, services run every 15 to 30 minutes between 5.57am and 11.27pm. A one-way ticket costs €8 and can be purchased from station ticket-vending machines.

Taxi

Taxi rides between Fiumicino and central Rome cost a fixed €48 for up to four passengers, including luggage. Taxis registered in Fiumicino charge more, so ensure you catch a Comune di Roma (Rome City Council) taxi (white with a Roma Capitale sign on the door). Journey time is usually between 45 and 60 minutes, depending on traffic.

CLIMATE

Rome has a Mediterranean climate, with hot summers and cool winters. Snow is rare. The best times to visit are between late March and early June, September and October, when the weather is mild and perfect for exploring the city. The wettest months are usually November and December.

TIME ZONE

Rome – like the rest of Italy – lies in the Western European time zone (GMT/UTC plus 1 hour), When it is 12pm in London, it is 1pm in Rome.

GETTING TO & FROM CIAMPINO AIRPORT

Ciampino is Rome's secondary airport, located 15 kilometres south-east of the city centre and serving mainly low-cost European carriers. Transport options include the following:

SIT Bus

Regular shuttle buses run between Ciampino and Stazione Termini (Via Marsala side). From the airport, buses depart every 30 to 60 minutes between 7.45am and 12.15am. From Termini, buses depart roughly every 30 to 60 minutes between 4.30am and 9.30pm. One-way tickets from Ciampino cost €5; one-way tickets from Termini cost €6. Tickets can be purchased onboard. Journey time is around 40 minutes, depending on traffic.

Schiaffini Rome Airport Bus

There are regular shuttle-bus services between the airport and Stazione Termini (Via Giolitti side). From the airport, buses depart every 30 to 65 minutes between 4am and 11.45pm. From Termini, buses run between 4.20am and 12am. One-way tickets cost €5.90 and can be purchased onboard.

Taxi

Taxis between Ciampino and central Rome cost a fixed €30 for up to four passengers, including luggage. Journey time is usually between 35 and 60 minutes, depending on traffic.

SAFETY

Rome is by and large a safe city, but it pays to follow some basic rules. Pickpockets are common, especially on crowded buses, metro trains, station platforms, major tourist sites and busy markets. Never store your wallet or other valuables in easy-to-reach pockets. Keep your bag closed and in sight. In case of theft or loss, always report the incident to the police within 24 hours and ask for a statement. On the street, ignore hagglers, no matter how charming or persistent.

GETTING AROUND THE CITY

Rome's public transport is operated by Atac (www.atac.roma.it) and tickets are valid on all city buses, metro trains and trams. A single ticket costs €1.50 and allows one metro ride or 100 minutes on all buses, including transfers. A one-day, unlimited-travel ticket costs €7; a 72-hour ticket is €18. Children under the age of 10 travel free. Purchase tickets before travel, either from a tabacchi (tobacconist) shop (denoted by a 'T') or from ticket-vending machines at metro stations and larger bus stops. Most machines take cash or card. On buses and trams, validate your ticket in the yellow-and-grey ticket validation machines. On the metro, validate at ticket barriers.

Bus

Buses are best for areas that the metro lines don't reach, including the heart of Rome's centro storico (historic centre). Most routes pass by Stazione Termini, with handy routes including the oft-crowded 40 and 64 connecting Termini to the city centre. Services generally run from 5.30am to 12am, with limited services running through the night. Enter buses from either front or back doors and always beware of pickpockets on crowded services.

Metro

Rome's limited metro network comprises three lines: A (orange), B (blue) and C (green). Trains run frequently from 5.30am to 11.30pm Sunday to Thursday, and to 1.30am Friday and Saturday nights. Lines A and B are most useful, crossing at Termini and reaching several important sights. Catch Line A for Basilica di San Giovanni Maggiore (San Giovanni), Trevi Fountain (Barberini), Spanish Steps (Spagna), and St Peter's Basilica and the Vatican Museums (Ottaviano-San Pietro). Catch Line B for the Colosseum and Roman Forum (Colosseo). Line C reaches Pigneto, crossing Line A at San Giovanni. When finally completed in the early 2020s, Line C will continue from San Giovanni to the Colosseum.

Tram

Rome's modest tram network is handy for reaching a handful of neighbourhoods, including Trastevere, Flaminio, Nomentana/Salario and Pigneto.

Taxi

Taxis are plentiful and can be caught at taxi ranks, by hailing one on the street or by booking ahead. Useful taxi-rank locations include Stazione Termini, Piazza Barberini, Piazza di Spagna, Pantheon, Largo di Torre Argentina, Colosseum and Piazza Pio XII. Use only officially licensed taxis, which are white and feature a 'Roman Capitale' sign on the doors and the taxi ID number. To book a taxi, call 06 06 09 or download the Chiamataxi app. Be aware that when you call for a taxi, the meter is switched on immediately, not once the taxi actually reaches you. Official taxi fares are listed at http://romamobilita.it/it/servizi/taxi/tariffe.

Walking

Central Rome is relatively compact and easily explored on foot. Invest in a comfortable pair of shoes and keep your eye out for dog droppings, which are all too common on the city's pavements.

MONEY & ATMS

- Italy's currency is the euro (€).
- Coins come in denominations of €1 and €2, as well as 1, 2, 5, 10, 20 and 50 cents. Notes come in denominations of €5, €10, €20, €50, €100, €200 and €500.
- A 22% IVA (value-added tax) is included in the price of most goods and services. Be mindful that all accommodation in Rome is subject to tassa di soggiorno (room-occupancy tax), charged on top of your bill (€3 to €7 per person per night depending on type of lodgings for a maximum of 10 consecutive nights).
- ATMs (bancomats) are widespread and most accept international cards. Major credit cards are widely accepted although some smaller and/or more traditional trattorias, hotels and shops may only accept cash.

PHONES & WI-FI

Rome's area code is 06 and must always be dialed, even if calling locally. To make an international call from Italy, dial 00, then the country and area codes of where you are calling, followed by the full number.

To avoid exorbitant roaming charges, consider buying an Italian prepaid SIM card (SIM prepagata). These can be used in European, Australian and unlocked US phones and are readily available from Italian telco stores for TIM (Telecom Italia Mobile; www.tim.it), Wind (www.wind.it), Vodafone (www.vodafone.it) and Tre (www.tre.it) networks. You will need to show your passport or ID card.

Free wi-fi is available at many cafes and bars, as well as in some museums, galleries and department stores. Most accommodation – including private Airbnb apartments – offer free wi-fi, although some top-tier hotels continue to charge for access.

Wifi Metropolitano (www.cittametropolitanaroma.gov.it/wifimetropolitano) offers numerous public wi-fi hotspots across the city. To use, you must first register online using a credit card or an Italian mobile phone. A wi-fi-hotspot map is available at www.mappawifi.cittametropolitanaroma.gov.it.

TIPPING

Italy does not have a strong tipping culture. That said, it's not uncommon to leave a small tip at sit-down eateries if servizio (service) is not included in your bill. As a general guide, leave a €1 or €2 tip at pizzerias and 10% of the total bill in restaurants. Porters at high-end hotels should be tipped about €5. Round off taxi fares to the nearest euro.

TOILETS

Public toilets are not especially easy to find, though you will find them at Stazione Termini (€1) and St Peter's Square. If you're out and nature calls, your easiest bet is to pop into a cafe or bar (though you should always purchase something as a courtesy). Toilets are common at museums and major department stores such as Rinascente.

SHOPPING TIPS

Non-EU residents who spend more than €155 at a single shop with a 'Tax Free' sign are eligible for a refund when leaving the EU. Ask the shop assistant for a tax-refund voucher, which needs to be filled in with the date of purchase and value. When leaving the EU, have the voucher stamped at customs and present it at the nearest tax-refund counter. The refund can be made in cash or transferred to your credit card. For more information, see www.taxrefund.it.

Everybody loves the saldi (sales). Winter sales usually run from early January to mid-February, while summer sales run from July to early September.

Most shops accept credit cards, though some smaller businesses and most market vendors only accept cash. Good-natured haggling is generally accepted at flea markets only.

WOMEN TRAVELLERS

While Rome is generally a safe destination, women may not always feel comfortable walking alone at night, especially in desolate areas, parks and the area around Termini train station. If you find yourself the victim of groping when in a crowded space, a loud Vergogna! – pronounced 'ver-gonya' and meaning 'Shame on you!' – should be enough to stop the offender.

LGBTQ TRAVELLERS

Homosexuality is legal in Italy and widely accepted in Rome, especially among younger generations. That said, the city remains conservative at heart and discretion is advised. The city's modest but popular 'gay district' consists of a couple of bars at the Colosseum end of Via di San Giovanni in Laterano. Queer-friendly clubs include Testaccio's long-running Alibi (Via di Monte Testaccio 44).

USEFUL WORDS & PHRASES

English is not as proficiently spoken in Rome as it is in some other European cities, but it is easy enough to get by with English alone. That said, knowing some basic Italian words and phrases is both handy and a good way to charm the locals.

Hello Ciao (informal), salve (polite)

Goodbye Arrivederci

Good morning Buon giorno

Good evening Buona sera

Good night Buona notte

How are you? Come stai? (informal) / Come sta? (polite)

I'm well, thanks. Sto bene, grazie.

Do you speak English? Parli inglese (informal) / Parla inglese? (polite)

I don't understand. Non capisco.

Nice to meet you. Molto lieto.

Please Per piacere / per favore

Thank you Grazie

Thank you very much Grazie mille

Excuse me Scusi

May I? Posso?

How much is this? Quanto costa?

Cheers! Salute! / Cin cin!

Delicious Buonissimo!

I'm full. Sono sazio. (male) / Sono sazia. (female)

Can I have the bill please? Il conto, per favore.

Airport Aeroporto

Station Stazione

Train Treno

Bus Autobus

Where do I need to get off? Dove devo scendere?

I love Rome/Italy! Amo Roma/l'Italia!

EATING & DRINKING

A trattoria is usually an informal, family-run restaurant focused on home-style regional cooking. A ristorante offers a more formal dining experience, with more elaborate regional or national dishes and more substantial wine list. An enoteca is a wine bar with grazing options and, in many cases, more substantial hot dishes. Many bars offer early evening, pre-dinner aperitivo, where your drink will come with complimentary snacks. Some bars offer generous aperitivo buffets, which can easily turn into one's budget-friendly dinner for the evening. Some local tips:

- Breakfast in Italy is usually little more than a cornetto (croissant) and caffè (coffee), consumed standing up at the local bar.

- Pasta is eaten with a fork, not a spoon.

- Pizza can be eaten with your hands.

- Eating bread with pasta is a no-no. Using bread to mop up any remaining sauce is encouraged.

- Avoid restaurants that come with a tourist menu (menù turistico), tout or prominent sign offering 'Free wi-fi'.

- It's always a good idea to call ahead to reserve a restaurant table, especially later in the week. Booking on the same day is usually fine. Call a few days ahead for popular places in peak season.

- At lunch and dinner, coffee is consumed after the meal, not with it.

- Most Italians only drink cappuccino or caffè latte in the morning. From midday, espresso is the coffee of choice. An espresso is simply called un caffè. Order a latte and you'll get a glass of milk. You will need to specify caffè latte for a milk coffee.

- Always make eye contact when toasting.

HOLIDAYS

Most Romans take their annual leave in August, when many escape al mare (to the beach) or in montagna (to the mountains). As a result, numerous shops and restaurants in the city close for a few weeks during this month. Official public holidays:

Capodanno (New Year's Day) 1 Jan

Epifania (Epiphany) 6 Jan

Pasquetta (Easter Monday) Mar/Apr

Giorno della Liberazione (Liberation Day) 25 Apr

Festa del Lavoro (Labour Day) 1 May

Festa della Repubblica (Republic Day) 2 June

Festa dei Santi Pietro e Paolo (Feast of St Peter & St Paul) 29 June

Ferragosto (Feast of the Assumption) 15 Aug

Festa di Ognisanti (All Saints' Day) 1 Nov

Festa dell'Immacolata Concezione (Feast of the Immaculate Conception) 8 Dec

Natale (Christmas Day) 25 Dec

Festa di Santo Stefano (Boxing Day) 26 Dec

FESTIVALS & EVENTS

To experience the city in celebratory mode, drop by during any of the following standout events:

Holy Week (Mar/Apr) The pope leads a candlelit procession around the Colosseum on Good Friday before blessing the masses in St Peter's Square on Easter Sunday.

Natale di Roma (Apr 21) Rome's annual birthday bash comes with live music, exhibitions, street parades, historical re-enactments and fireworks.

Open House Roma (May; www.openhouseroma. org) Offers access to hundreds of notable buildings, usually closed to the public, over one weekend, plus free guided tours.

Gay Village (late June to early Sept; www. gayvillage.it) Ten weeks of festival bars, restaurants and queer culture, from film screenings, theatre and music to seminars and dance parties.

Romaeuropa Festival (late Sept to early Dec; www.romaeuropa.net) An impressive program of theatre, dance and opera featuring top-tier Italian and international artists.

Festa del Cinema di Roma (Oct; www. romacinemafest.it) Rome's major film fest spans 11 days, with world premieres, retrospectives, panels, master classes and star power.

ABOUT THE AUTHOR

Born to northern Italian parents, Australian travel writer Cristian Bonetto spends significant amounts of time in Italy each year. While he loathes playing favourites, he will admit that Rome has a particular hold on him. Not only does he love its nail-biting backstory, extraordinary architecture and ivy-clad back streets, he's also drawn to its less obvious, everyday charms, from vintage espresso bars to avant-garde concept stores, off-the-radar boutiques and suburban street art. Together, they keep his camera clicking and his notebooks full of scribbles and stories.

Cristian began his writing life as a playwright, running a small theatre company and producing a handful of comedies. In 2003, his play *Il Cortile* (The Courtyard) was awarded an Australia Council grant and was performed in numerous Italian cities, including Rome. After a short stint writing scripts for Australian soaps *Home & Away* and *Neighbours* in the early 2000s, Cristian turned his hand to travel writing. Since 2006, he has written more than 30 travel guides for Lonely Planet, for destinations as varied as Naples, Venice, Copenhagen, New York, Los Angeles, Singapore and Brisbane. He is also a globe-trotting host of travel videos and a travel writer for UK newspaper *The Telegraph*.

ACKNOWLEDGEMENTS

Many people helped make this book happen. First and foremost, grazie mille to series creator Melissa Kayser for entrusting me with the first edition of *Rome Precincts*. Also, a huge grazie to Megan Cuthbert for her guidance, and to Susan Paterson for toning and tweaking my work to make it the best it can be.

On the ground, I'm forever grateful to the old friends, new friends and strangers who generously shared their tips, insights and fresh perspectives on the city. Special thanks to Alberto Puoti, Elisabetta Quagliato and Massimo Quagliato, Sabrina Crawford, Gloria Gobbi and Maya N'Diaye, Barbara Lessona, Andrea Giurato and Cristina Delli Fiori, Abigail Blasi and Elif Emine Sallorenzo, Joe Brizzi, Massimiliano Rubcich, Duncan Garwood, Elisia Menduni, Cristina Bowerman, Livia Hengel and Diletta Ruta.

Back home, a huge thank you to my family and friends for their support, love and patience. A special 'grazie' to Donna Wheeler for her seasoned tips. Last, but never least, thank *you*, for choosing me as your guide through the Città Eterna.

PHOTOGRAPHY CREDITS

All photography © Cristian Bonetto except the following:

Back cover: Stocksy
Title page: Alessandro Rossetti
p. 002 (top): Co. Ro. Jewels
p. 018 (bottom): Blind Eye Factory
p. 042 (top): Serena Eller
p. 048: Alessandro Rossetti
p. 136: Francesca Metta and Agnese Consoorsi
p. 181: Massimiliano Rubcich
p. 208: Lorna Davidson
p. 213 (top): Mary Stuart
p. 231: Barbara Lessons

Published in 2019 by Hardie Grant Travel, a division of Hardie Grant Publishing

Hardie Grant Travel (Melbourne)
Building 1, 658 Church Street
Richmond, Victoria 3121

Hardie Grant Travel (Sydney)
Level 7, 45 Jones Street
Ultimo, NSW 2007

www.hardiegrant.com/au/travel

A catalogue record for this book is available from the National Library of Australia

Rome Precincts
ISBN 9781741175561

10 9 8 7 6 5 4 3 2 1

Publisher
Melissa Kayser

Senior editor
Megan Cuthbert

Editor
Susan Paterson

Editorial assistance
Rosanna Dutson

Proofreader
Alice Barker

Cartographer
Emily Maffei

Design
Michelle Mackintosh

Typesetting
Megan Ellis

Index
Max McMaster

Prepress
Megan Ellis and Splitting Image Colour Studio

Printed and bound in China by LEO Paper Group

A free digital download of the text and maps from this book is available at: https://goo.gl/RqkKdG
Just make sure to have this book handy, so you can answer some questions as proof of purchase.